Winning in the Virtual Workplace

10 Experts Reveal How to Lead Your Remote Team to Success

Editors

Brian M. Allen, Marie Bakari, John Frame, Linda Larsen, Stephanie Menefee, Melody Rawlings, Kathy Richie, Randee L. Sanders, and Gary White

National UNIVERSITY | CENTER FOR THE ADVANCEMENT OF VIRTUAL ORGANIZATIONS

Center for the Advancement of Virtual Organizations

National University's Center for the Advancement of Virtual Organizations (CAVO) is a hub of relevant resources providing current information and practices to support professionals and educators in various industries involved in remote work. Serving as a collaborative platform, CAVO partners with remote work experts to integrate research and practical knowledge, with the goal of disseminating the latest developments and technologies associated with remote work. For podcast episodes and other resources to help you lead a virtual organization, please visit: https://www.nu.edu/center-advancement-virtual-organizations.

Contents

Introduction: The Virtual Leadership Framework

Melody Rawlings and John Frame

This book provides a collection of chapters to help you improve your knowledge of the world of remote and hybrid work. The Virtual Leadership Framework (see Figure 1) is used to structure insights from ten experts on virtual work, delivering strategies to help you thrive and be successful in your remote workplace. Each section of this book aligns with one of the components of the framework, as explored below.

The Virtual Leadership Framework is a model devised by colleagues from the Center for the Advancement of Virtual Organizations (CAVO) to help us better conceptualize important concepts relevant to virtual organizations. As shown in Figure 1, it is comprised of six components (Emotional

Intelligence, Communication, Engagement, Accountability, Human Capital, and Continuous Improvement). The central component of the framework is Emotional Intelligence, which is foundational to each of the other five components.

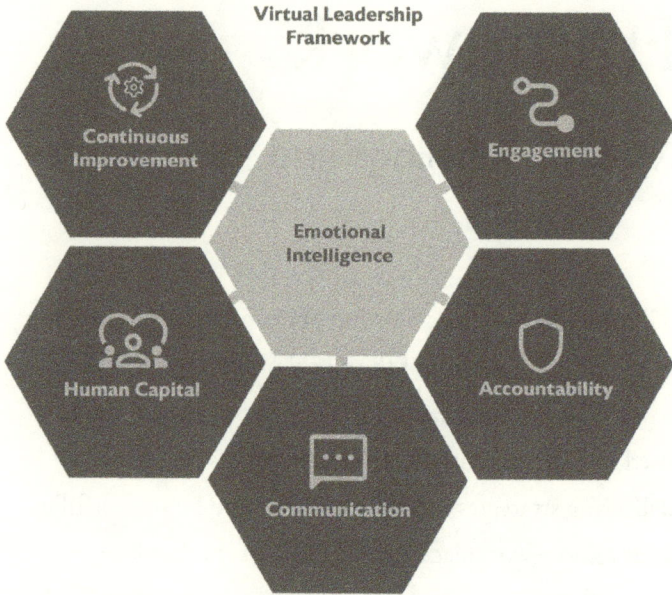

Figure 1 - The Virtual Leadership Framework

Drawing from the work by Rawlings et al. (2020), each of the six components of the Virtual Leadership Framework is briefly described below (Lubich et al., 2022).

Emotional Intelligence

Emotional Intelligence is at the heart of the Virtual Leadership Framework, as it plays a significant role in leadership effectiveness (Goleman, 1998) and in the other five components of the framework. Emotional Intelligence enables leaders to understand and manage emotions. Leaders with high Emotional Intelligence thoughtfully manage interpersonal relationships and are more likely to pick up on the feelings of others and, when needed, adapt their communication for better understanding (Pitts et al., 2012). Virtual leaders need a heightened awareness of their employees' emotions, paying close attention to indications of potential issues or concerns.

Communication

Effective communication plays a vital role in virtual and hybrid workplaces, and it's crucial to be mindful of what we convey through our formal and informal communication. In virtual and hybrid workplaces, employees and stakeholders depend heavily on electronic communication, making it essential to grasp the concept of netiquette (the practice of showing courtesy and respect in online interactions).

Virtual leaders and managers should establish guidelines for considerate communication and behavior to foster a comfortable, efficient, and inclusive online atmosphere. Furthermore, implementing a communication strategy for virtual teams can significantly help in reducing potential conflicts.

Engagement

Promoting engagement, dedication, and trust among virtual employees is essential for improving efficiency and developing a culture that fosters meaningful relationships. This can be accomplished through several approaches, including consistently checking in with your team, building community through social events, and ensuring all voices are valued.

Accountability

Establishing accountability in the virtual workplace is crucial. This can be done by defining explicit goals, expectations, policies, and procedures, and employing realistic metrics to measure performance.

Virtual leaders must be competent and available. Being present in the virtual environment is crucial for overseeing team dynamics and progress, and it reassures team members of our availability to assist and support the team in achieving their objectives.

Human Capital

An organization's human capital is the unique strengths and qualities employees bring to the table. It includes what they know, what they can do, and their personality traits, all of which add value to the organization. Important to consider with human capital are the concepts of motivation, diversity and inclusivity, worker development, talent acquisition and development, and work/life balance.

Continuous Improvement

Continuous improvement refers to the ongoing effort to enhance business processes, products, or services. It includes considering change management and adopting an appreciative inquiry approach, emphasizing strengths rather than weaknesses, and recognizing accomplishments and building upon them. Additionally, Continuous Improvement is being aware of issues related to risk mitigation, as well as business continuity, as the success of an organization hinges on its capacity to sustain operations during times of difficulty.

Altogether, these six components (Emotional Intelligence, Communication, Engagement, Accountability, Human Capital, and Continuous Improvement) make up the Virtual Leadership Framework—a model to help guide leaders across diverse industries to develop and maintain an effective virtual workplace. Let's now look at the organization of this book, beginning with Emotional Intelligence in the first chapter.

⊷⊷ ·◆· ⊶⊶

Chapter Topics

Emotional Intelligence is at the core of the Virtual Leadership Framework and is a vital thread that runs through each of the framework's other components. Therefore, we begin the book with this important topic. In chapter 1, author and speaker Sylvia Baffour explores leading with Emotional Intelligence. Sylvia, a Certified Psychological Safety Coach with experience helping individuals and organizations, tells us about four practices (fostering psychological safety, managing emotions, building trust and influence, and demonstrating empathy) related to Emotional Intelligence that support leaders of virtual organizations to cultivate engagement and collaboration among employees. Sylvia includes practical tips with each of these four practices, including a couple for building our "empathy muscles."

Moving forward and looking into each of the other components of the Virtual Leadership Framework, we begin with Communication in chapter 2, where Lauren Sergy provides specific guidance on how to have great virtual meetings. She gives a variety of tips, including how to appear well on camera, such as by using gestures and making eye contact. Lauren is an expert in interpersonal communication in the workplace, supporting people to become more effective leaders through skilled communication. She believes that virtual work requires learned skills, and her chapter provides lots of insight to help us in our virtual meetings.

Continuing to explore the Communication component of the Virtual Leadership Framework, in chapter 3 we hear from Molly Gutterud, who is a marketing and communications professional specializing in digital strategy and brand management. Molly also provides insight into communication in virtual organizations, offering strategies to help leaders in this area. She introduces a four-part communication framework (based on the four Cs of culture, content, consistency, and collaboration) that can help those in virtual organizations communicate more effectively.

In the next chapter, we turn a corner and begin exploring the area of Engagement, hearing from Elizabeth Kemp Caulder, who specializes in the field of brand marketing, and who founded The Phoenix Lifestyle Marketing Group. Elizabeth, who emphasizes the value of remote work—and not just for the benefit of employees, but also for organizations—offers five tips (using T.E.A.M.S. as an acronym) to help leaders of virtual organizations. One of the things she writes is, "Engaging consistently and transparently is paramount to ensuring that your team members feel that they are part of a larger whole, and that they can trust you, as well."

Continuing the theme of Engagement, in chapter 5 Geraldine Woloch-Addamine reminds us about the importance of employee recognition, connecting this with employee engagement. She comes to this topic from her role as founder and CEO of Good4work, a Total Talent Recognition software that aims to increase engagement and recognition in the workplace. In her chapter, Geraldine emphasizes the value of recognition and its connection to motivation and a positive working environment.

Following this, we look at issues related to the theme of Accountability. In chapter 6, we hear from Anand Madhavan, who holds an MBA and has vast experience at Gallup as the Director of Digital Strategy. Along with presenting charts showing data related to remote working, Anand explores accountability and the importance of a good leader. He writes, "To sustain accountability and productivity in a hybrid or remote world, it takes ownership between the organization, managers, and employees."

Chapter 7 is written by Nadia Harris, who holds a legal degree specializing in remote work law and is an expert in international remote and hybrid work. Nadia introduces us to the concept of proximity bias—an important issue in the world of virtual work—including consequences of this type of bias (if office-based workers are looked on more highly than remote employees). She argues for the need to spread awareness about proximity bias and ensure objectivity in the workplace.

In chapter 8, by William J. Quinn, III, an operations and project management professional with vast experience in the field of manufacturing, we begin examining the topic of Human Capital. More specifically, William explores project management in the virtual workplace, providing tips in the areas of communication, time management, organizational awareness, problem-solving, and leadership. He wisely advises, "To succeed as a project manager, you need to put at least as much time and energy into connecting with your people as you do on the project itself."

We continue the theme on Human Capital in chapter 9, hearing from Catherine Mattiske, in the first of her two chapters included in this book. Catherine, who specializes in corporate learning and team building, has served clients in many different industries, helping strengthen teams and improve results. In this chapter, she discusses connection, communication, and influence—three of the four concepts in what she calls the "Genius Quotient" model—a framework to help virtual teams achieve success. Throughout the chapter, Catherine provides practical guidance for virtual leaders related to each of these three concepts.

In the following chapter, we look at the last component of the Virtual Leadership Framework, Continuous Improvement. Catherine Mattiske continues exploring the Genius Quotient model that she introduced in chapter 10, focusing on the fourth of the model's four concepts, Learn. In this chapter, Catherine connects learning, continuous improvement, and having a growth mindset.

Finally, Cristina Imre, an executive coach, entrepreneur, and business strategist with vast remote work experience, concludes the book, providing an overview of several concepts related to the world of virtual work, including its benefits and challenges. She also looks at current and future technology and tools for remote work, and concludes, "By embracing the challenges and opportunities associated with remote work, we can create a future in which people are free to work from anywhere, revolutionizing urban planning and transportation, the global economy and job market, company culture, employee well-being, and society."

Together, these ten experts bring insights that can help us as we serve those in our virtual work environments. You may wish to dip in and out of this book, focusing on the topics that are of most interest to you. Our hope is that you take away knowledge for your leadership journey that will not only help you and your virtual organization, but also the wider field of remote work.

References

Goleman, D. (1998). What makes a leader? *Harvard Business Review, 76,* 93–104.

Lubich, K. K., Rawlings, M., & Menefee, S. S. (2022). Emotional intelligence and virtual leadership: A framework and pathway forward. *International Leadership Journal, 14*(1), 77-86.

Pitts, V. E., Wright, N. A., & Harkabus, L. C. (2012). Communication in virtual teams: The role of emotional intelligence. *Journal of Organizational Psychology, 12*(3/4), 21.

Rawlings, M., Menefee, S., White, G., & Allen, B. (2020). Center for the Advancement of Virtual Organizations. Na-

tional University. https://www.nu.edu/center-advancemen
t-virtual-organizations.

Section I – Emotional Intelligence

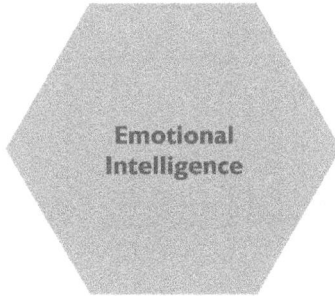

Emotional Intelligence

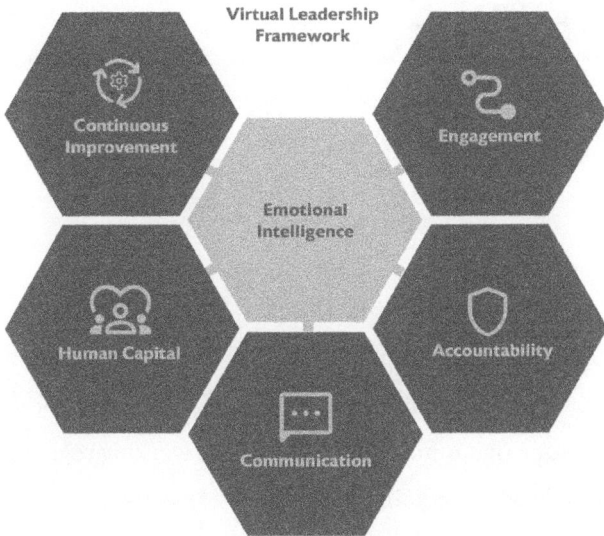

Virtual Leadership Framework

Continuous Improvement

Engagement

Emotional Intelligence

Human Capital

Accountability

Communication

Chapter One

Practical Tips for Leading Distributed Workspaces with Emotional Intelligence

Sylvia Baffour

I t's no secret the way we work has changed. Thriving and succeeding as an organization in a remote/virtual or hybrid world requires an emotionally intelligent workforce—one that is filled with individuals working together effectively while building positive relationships and creating a supportive and productive work environment. In a distributed work environment, leaders will need to harness critical skills to enhance collaboration, manage change or conflict, build trust, and navigate work relationships in the absence of in-person interactions.

If you have an opportunity to lead teams within a distributed work environment, you can leverage emotional intelligence (EI) to help you thrive in your leadership role by keeping the following four EI practices in mind.

EI Practice #1 – Contribute to Your Team's Psychological Safety

By their very nature, remote or hybrid work environments tend to have teams that feel less connected and less collaborative and have less of a sense of belonging. Some of this is due to fewer opportunities to have casual "water-cooler" conversations, read body language and nonverbal cues, and connect with others in reassuring ways when feelings such as imposter syndrome surface. This can adversely affect your team's effectiveness as they struggle to feel psychologically safe.

Building a psychologically safe culture ought to be an intentional practice. While you may be the leader, it should not be left to you alone. It takes a team effort, with you leading the way, for each member to contribute in such an environment. Ultimately, you want to create a supportive, inclusive work environment that encourages collaboration, trust, and open communication. Embracing the following four habits will ensure you're building more psychological safety into your remote/virtual or hybrid work culture.

Habit #1 – Commit to More Transparency about the Challenges You Face

It's often believed that to be an effective, influential leader, you must always show strength with those you lead. If the past couple of years has taught us anything, it is that gone are the days when leaders could keep things close to their chest while leaving their teams in the dark and still expect them to perform at a high level. We've learned that what individuals on teams want most is to be led by someone who allows their own humanity to shine through in everything they do.

Showing more of your humanity can help you build stronger relationships with those you lead, inspiring a healthier, more positive, and supportive work environment. At the end of the day, isn't that what effective leadership is all about? As you confront day-to-day work challenges, how often are you seeking additional help or admitting when you don't know something? When you show you are vulnerable, including sharing aspects of your personal life, it humanizes you and helps your team better relate to you. And this is exactly what you need to build trust and lead a more collaborative and engaged team.

The key is to strike a healthy balance between how many of your vulnerabilities you share and the boundaries you set to ensure that you're still presenting a professional front. Realize that you are leading human beings who show up each day (no matter where they're working from), carrying the challenges and obstacles they face in their personal lives. If they are expected to "check all that at the door," they will begin to feel less loyalty and enthusiasm to show up each day to give their best. When they experience you sharing more of yourself and allow themselves to feel seen and heard by you, they will bring more of themselves to work each day. Your actions will inspire loyalty and collaboration, and minimize feelings of disconnection.

Habit #2 – Make Room for the Differences in Others

Recognize that every one of your team members brings with them unique experiences and perspectives. It's vital to avoid using a blanket-style or one-size-fits-all leadership approach when dealing with them. For instance, while some on your team may be "straight-shooters" with the ability to absorb direct, "unsweetened" feedback from you, others may be more sensitive and require a gentler approach when it comes to your choice of words with them.

Leading by example with respect to acknowledging and appreciating the uniqueness of your team members will set the stage for them to support you as you create a welcoming and inclusive work environment. They will also be watching to see how well you foster open communication, promote diversity and inclusion, and address conflict constructively. This matters most, especially as you lead individuals who may not work in the same geographical location.

Think about all the ways you can show your team members you appreciate their individuality and unique contributions. As you think about this, consider some of these questions to help you be more intentional in your efforts to make room for others on your team to feel appreciated:

- Do I encourage team members to express their opinions and perspectives, and actively listen to what they have to say?

- Do I prioritize diversity, inclusion, and belonging in our workplace, and encourage my team to celebrate and learn from each other's differences?

- Am I fostering an environment where my team can understand and empathize with each other, and everyone feels valued and respected?

- When conflicts arise, do I help my team find a resolution that respects everyone's differences and perspectives?

Habit #3 – Share Constant and Constructive Feedback with Your Team

As we grow and develop along our professional paths, we will most likely experience, at one point or another, some imposter syndrome. That feeling of uncertainty might leave your team members thinking they're out of their league or not deserving of the accomplishments they've achieved. To pile on top of that, we know that working in distributed workspaces can often feel isolating, with a chance that, from time to time, employees may feel a greater sense of self-doubt or inadequacy.

Since you are their leader, your ability to communicate as openly as possible is not just reassuring for your team members, it is paramount if you want to build and maintain a culture of trust, transparency, and psychological safety. Those you lead deserve to know as often as possible where they stand in terms of their performance. When you're committed to providing constant and constructive feedback to your team (done with care), it solidifies your connection to each of them and helps you build a strong, happy, and productive team that feels seen, valued, and supported, even while contributing from distributed workspaces. Here are three additional benefits to sharing feedback more openly and honestly.

Increased motivation – When your feedback helps enlighten individuals about how they're doing, that can be motivating for them as they get a sense of their progress.

Greater effectiveness – Your feedback plays a vital role in helping them better understand their strengths and opportunities for growth, and this lays down a clear path for their development on your team.

Productive and successful relationships – Your openness and transparency in communicating constant feedback will help you build stronger relationships with those you lead and foster a sense of trust and mutual understanding.

Habit #4 – Incorporate Meaningful Virtual Team Building Rituals

You might agree with the growing sentiment that the barrage of virtual meetings has taken the fun out of team gatherings. People working remotely may grapple with added interruptions, including from family, and the convenience of hosting virtual meetings means that people are being flooded with more meetings than necessary.

As a leader, if you have no choice but to conduct your meetings virtually, bringing a bit of fun and liveliness to your virtual gatherings is important. And while virtual rituals aren't a cure-all, they can help your team feel more connected and have more of a sense of belonging—all of which contribute meaningfully to a healthy culture. Consider these ideas for your virtual team building rituals:

Virtual coffee/tea chats – Give your team some time to relax and casually connect with each other virtually without the need for formalities or a set agenda. Allow them free rein to chat about things ranging from work-related matters to personal interests and hobbies. This is a great way to promote remote team building and serves to keep employees connected, maintaining social connections while working remotely.

Meaningful check-ins – Consider developing a routine to spend a few minutes (even as little as five or ten minutes) before your meeting begins, engaging your team in a conversation about something interesting that happened to them, or some fun observation they can share with others. During this allotted time, encourage them to talk about things other than work.

Virtual brainstorming – Get your team in the habit of thinking creatively and bouncing ideas off each other to encourage greater collaboration. Take advantage of the fact that employees can bring their diverse experiences and ideas to the table without the need for travel or scheduling conflicts.

To get the most out of these brainstorming sessions, encourage team members to submit their ideas anonymously and ensure the group takes time to discuss each idea. Doing this ensures that everyone feels heard and team decisions are evaluated on their strength and viability instead of simply on who they come from.

Virtual games – Encourage employees to join you in playing games, such as Pictionary or trivia, to help build camaraderie and connection with each other. You can also take advantage of a platform like Kahoot to create categories that reflect your team's interests or work-related topics and offer prizes for the winning team. Additionally, you can consider fun and challenging team-building activities such as Escape Hunt, a virtual escape room. It offers your team a chance to work together to solve puzzles and clues to escape a virtual room.

EI Practice #2 – Engage Your Emotions Wisely

Having emotions and the ability to express them is a big part of what makes us human. Each day, you get to choose whether you will use your emotions to work for you or against you. This means that even in moments when you are negatively triggered by something or someone, you still have the power to manage what you do about how you're feeling. And what you choose to do can make all the difference to those in your line of impact.

As someone leading a team in distributed workspaces, being aware and in control of your emotions is vital. While you may experience a wide array of emotions as you move through each day, it's important to remember that your emotions are neither good nor bad. They are simply signals to indicate how you're feeling about something happening to or around you. What you choose to do about how you feel is what has the potential to create positive or negative outcomes.

Consider this example. You find yourself angered by an email a team member sends you. How does that make you feel, and what do you do about it? Do you give yourself some time to think purposefully about your response, or do you react immediately and send a reply based on how you're feeling at that moment? I invite you to pause and reflect on that briefly. The reality is that in a virtual/remote or hybrid work environment, words typed in an email carry more weight because they travel across communication lines without the benefit of verbal cues or body language. For this reason, it is important to engage your emotions wisely when triggered. Here are three strategies to help ensure you're using your emotions to work in your favor:

Strategy #1 – Practice a Thirty-Second Pause

While it might feel easier said than done, there is always an opportunity for you to create a few seconds of space between the moment you're triggered and when you choose to respond. As a leader, whenever you act impulsively to being triggered emotionally, it takes away your power to influence the outcome in your favor. As famed comedian Jim Carrey once said, "The effect you have on others is the most valuable currency there is" (Carrey, 2017). And I suggest that if it is a good effect you have on those you lead, it buys you favor, loyalty, influence, and much more.

Consider deliberately pausing for thirty seconds every time you feel agitating emotions such as anger, fear, frustration, overwhelm, or helplessness. Those precious seconds will allow you time to center yourself and bring more thought and less impulse to the moment. As you keep practicing the thirty-second pause, you will find yourself reacting more wisely to things that trigger you. Those around you will inevitably benefit from your level-headed leadership, most especially in times of stress and frustration.

Strategy #2 – Hone Your Hunch

One of the biggest benefits of giving yourself a few seconds of pause when triggered, is that it gives you a chance to examine your assumptions (a.k.a. your hunch). We all tend to make assumptions about people's intentions or about circumstances we find ourselves in, and often those assumptions are rarely positive. We imagine the worst of intentions in others, and that influences how we feel and what we choose to do next.

Let's revisit the example of the triggering email you received from a team member. The moment after you read it, stop and ask yourself whether you are assuming positive intent or the worst-case scenario. If your default is to assume that they meant to be rude, demanding, offensive, or some other undesirable behavior, you're more likely to fly off the handle and react impulsively. This could result in you sending a reply that you later wish you could unsend.

While pausing for those thirty seconds, if you become more mindful of the kinds of assumptions you're making at that moment, it will help you create space for more compassion or patience about the situation, because you realize that there might be another side to the story. Ultimately, that precious pause will empower you to have a more composed response to the email.

Strategy #3 – Adopt Shifting Phrases

In addition to consciously taking a thirty-second pause and "honing your hunch" about the situation, you can also engage your emotions wisely by adopting what I call "Shifting Phrases." This is a kind of self-talk that allows you to lower the temperature of the emotion you might be feeling, while keeping you level-headed throughout the triggering moment. These phrases ultimately help you rein in those impulsive instincts and judgments. For example, if you feel ignored (an emotional trigger), rather than thinking, *They deliberately excluded me from that meeting*, you can shift to, *Could there be a reason I'm unaware of for why I wasn't included in the meeting?* By using Shifting Phrases, you can heighten the chance that your emotions will work for you and not against you.

There is bad and good news about emotional triggers. Your emotional triggers may always be a trigger for you (the bad news). But, how you choose to be affected by your triggers is what can change and be improved over time (the good news). Perhaps you're someone who will always be triggered by what feels like a condescending conversation. While that may be the case, over time you can become less adversely affected by tense conversations. How? By injecting some Shifting Phrases into your mind to help you avoid making assumptions that pull you away from being in control of what you do next.

I understand that it can be difficult to maintain a sense of calm when juggling a work deadline and a weekly calendar full of meetings and/or ongoing family obligations. And I know that, from time to time, your emotions will threaten to send you over the edge. Yet, it is still important to do what you can to engage your emotions wisely.

The truth of the matter is that, while you cannot control your initial thought when triggered, you are responsible for your second thought, as well as the first action you take. So, when triggered, exercise prudence and center yourself back to a place where you can bring your best self to the interaction. Use Shifting Phrases to help you manage your emotional triggers effectively.

EI Practice #3 — Mind Your Emotional Aftertaste

If you're like most leaders leading distributed teams, you want to have a positive influence on them, no matter where they are located and how much or how little you interact with them. Having a positive influence makes your life easier and increases the quality of your collaborations and overall team productivity.

The bottom line is that every interaction you have with others, whether you are aware of it or not, leaves behind an emotional aftertaste—the feeling others get as a result of interacting with you. Often, that feeling is either sweet or sour.

While you cannot *control* how those you lead feel about you (and it's not your job to control that), you do indeed have the power to *influence* how you make them feel. That power to influence can be especially important with your remote interactions and communications.

Let's look at three of the most practical ways to positively influence the emotional aftertaste of your interactions. Incorporate these strategies into your leadership style and watch how they positively inspire and influence your team members:

Strategy #1 – Focus on the Emotions You Want to Create in Others

You may be the kind of leader who takes time to process or pre-plan your thoughts before meeting with someone, to ensure a meaningful and productive interaction. But how often do you stop to think about *what* you want the other person to feel once your encounter or conversation has ended? It's amazing how much we can influence the emotions of others by paying special attention to our word choices and overall communication style.

Consider a scenario where you must deliver constructive feedback to a direct report who is loyal and enthusiastic but needs to improve in a couple of important areas. Thinking in advance of your interaction and *what* you want them to feel will greatly influence your choice of words in communicating with them. Maybe you want them to feel hopeful and inspired to step up and give their best. Keeping this in mind as you formulate your thoughts will ensure you're using language that feels hopeful and inspirational. Remember that in a remote environment, your words matter more than ever.

Strategy #2 – Be Present as You Interact

One of the most fundamental human desires we all have is the need to feel seen, heard and valued. In this very distracting and multitasking world we live in, the more present you can be in all your interactions, the greater your chances of connecting effectively with others. When you give someone your undivided attention, it greatly enhances the chance that they will feel heard, even in moments when you might disagree.

The next time you engage with a team member, pay attention to how present you are. Are you listening to them actively or passively while awaiting your turn to talk? Be mindful of your own thoughts and feelings, as well as the emotions of those around you. Think about what you can do to practice being present in the moment, rather than getting caught up in worries or distractions.

Part of being present for your team means being there for them when they need you, and showing empathy when they are going through a difficult time. However, avoid the trap of thinking that you must resolve every problem or challenge disclosed to you. Empathy is simply about allowing people to feel seen and heard, even if you can't help them solve their issue. They will greatly appreciate you for listening earnestly, and that creates feelings of trust, connection, and psychological safety.

Strategy #3 – Listen with More Curiosity and Less Judgment

In general, we tend to judge people and situations more often than we are curious about them. Think about the last time a judgment crept into your mind. Did you run with the thoughts you had at that moment, or did you stop to say something like, "I wonder why I am thinking this about this person or situation."

We probably don't inject curiosity enough into the very moments it's most needed. As a leader leading teams in distributed workspaces, curiosity is a skill that can have a transformative impact on your leadership effectiveness. It helps enhance your work relationships and increase employee engagement. Being curious requires you to pay special attention to the quality of questions you ask those you lead. So, ask thoughtful questions.

Do your questions close off a conversation, giving people the impression that you're not open to their ideas? Or do your conversations include open-ended questions that invite others to be reflective and engage in a meaningful discussion?

Asking open-ended questions helps the other person feel as though you're interested in what they think because your question is structured in such a way that it invites them to elaborate on their thought or idea. As an example, a closed question could be, "Do you think this is a good idea?" Typically, closed questions can be answered with just one word like *yes* or *no*. Open-ended questions invite more conversation and could be something like "How would you approach this situation?" or "Why might this be a good idea to pursue?"

While caring about the quality of questions you ask is important, you must also pay attention to how your questions can influence the response you receive. Beware of the trap of confirmation bias that will have you asking questions in a way that simply serves to seek out agreement from others. Instead, lean into your questions with genuine curiosity and avoid phrasing things in a way that makes them feel like a foregone conclusion.

Empower your remote/virtual or hybrid team to have their own opinions and share their perspectives. Encourage their growth and learning, while creating a safe space for them to showcase their own leadership. Doing this assists you in building a team of thinkers who bring fresh ideas and the kind of problem-solving that helps you create more successful outcomes.

EI Practice #4 – Relate to Your Team with Greater Empathy

As human beings, we're hard-wired for connection and none of us succeeds in life alone. We exist in relation to one another, and so it's imperative to care about building trust and cultivating meaningful collaborations with others.

We've all endured discomfort and uncertainty. Now more than ever, as we show up to work each day, we want to feel valued and feel that our contributions matter. Teams in distributed workspaces tend toward a need to feel seen and valued, especially because their work environment can feel more isolated.

As a leader, it's important for you to understand that the skill of empathy is at the heart of what helps you create a healthy and productive virtual/remote or hybrid work culture—one where people feel seen and valued even from a distance. As we dive deeper into what it takes to build up our "empathy muscles," we'll explore three of the most effective ways to do so, namely, Perspective-Taking, Perspective-Getting, and the 2-by-2 Rule.

Empathy Muscle Builder #1 – Practice Perspective-Taking

There's a common misperception that showing empathy to others is about being nice or about agreeing with someone's viewpoint. The reality is that empathy is far from that. It's all about allowing others to feel seen and heard, even if we disagree. Perspective-taking is foundational to helping others feel understood, by earnestly considering their viewpoint, feelings, beliefs, and thoughts. While we are not expected to step into someone else's shoes perfectly, we are invited to try our best to see the world from their perspective.

As a leader in a hybrid/remote workspace, this is a valuable skill that will enhance your relationships, because it allows you to empathize, communicate more effectively, and build stronger connections with your fellow team members. You may also experience the added benefit of better problem-solving and decision-making, as it allows you to consider different options and anticipate potential outcomes.

Taking on other people's perspectives is a skill you can develop through intentional practice. How? By actively listening to others without judgment to better understand their thoughts and emotions. Staying open to the diverse opinions and perspectives of others is also key to effective perspective-taking.

Empathy Muscle Builder #2 — Embrace Perspective-Getting

While perspective-taking involves listening without judgment to imagine what it is like to be in someone else's shoes, perspective-getting focuses on gaining a different point of view of a situation by *asking* others about their experience. It involves considering different viewpoints and opinions and seeking to understand the nuances and complexities of a situation.

Engaging in perspective-getting can happen in various ways, including dialoguing with people with different views, reading about a topic from different sources, or simply reflecting on one's biases and assumptions. In cultivating more empathy, perspective-getting aims to broaden our understanding of a topic or situation, to gain a more nuanced and informed perspective. This helps prevent narrow-minded thinking, biases, and stereotyping. As you seek out different perspectives, you are more likely to appreciate the diversity of your team's experiences and ideas, and make more informed decisions based on a wider range of information.

In a nutshell, both of the above pathways to empathy are valuable and worthy of embracing and practicing. The main distinction between the two is this: perspective-taking involves imagining yourself in another person's situation, while perspective-getting involves actively gathering information about another person's perspective through direct communication or observation.

Empathy Muscle Builder #3 – Adopt the 2-by-2 Rule

It is understandable that, as a leader, there are some decisions you need to make behind closed doors. Remember, though, the teams you're leading in distributed workspaces can feel isolated and left in the dark about a lot of decisions that may ultimately impact them. Being as transparent and accountable as possible will serve you well when it comes to your effectiveness as a leader. You cannot build a psychologically safe culture where your team members feel mutual trust and a sense of belonging if you aren't deliberate about how you help them feel seen, heard, and valued.

As you make decisions moving forward, I invite you to adopt the 2-by-2 Rule. This is a rule that requires you to ask yourself (and answer) two vital questions before you make decisions that impact others:

1. What are two reasons someone might *agree* with my decision?

2. What are two reasons someone might *disagree* with
   my decision?

Make a habit of using this 2-by-2 Rule and you will find
yourself injecting more empathy into your decision-making.
Why? Because you force yourself to imagine the perspective of
someone who has a different opinion from yours. Thinking
about that can enlighten you to their viewpoint or at least
help you appreciate their alternate perspective. Even if you
end up sticking with your own decision, they will have felt
heard and understood along the way.

Final Thoughts

Leading others in a remote/virtual or hybrid work environment can indeed present unique challenges that make it feel
more difficult than leading individuals in a traditional work
environment. The lack of physical presence can make it harder to establish a strong team culture and a sense of community; however, achieving this is still possible. Leverage the emotional intelligence practices we've discussed to help you overcome some of the challenges of leading a distributed workforce. As you incorporate them into your leadership style,
you will be well on your way to building and maintaining an
emotionally intelligent workforce that collaborates effectively
for the greater good of your team and organization.

References

Carrey, J. (2017, September 17). *Jim Carrey's 5 most inspiring speeches.* [Speech audio recording]. *Newsweek.* https://www.newsweek.com/jim-carrey-inspiring-speeches-663453

Section II – Communication

Virtual Leadership Framework

Chapter Two

Speaking Through the Webcam: Understanding Virtual as a Unique Medium of Communication

Lauren Sergy

When the COVID-19 pandemic triggered widespread lockdowns in early 2020, it also ushered in a rapid mainstreaming of virtual meeting platforms. While the adoption of virtual communication platforms and remote work had been steadily increasing pre-pandemic, there were still plenty who didn't see it as a viable part of their operations. Suddenly, organizations who had previously resisted the widespread adoption of virtual communication were dragged—sometimes kicking and screaming—into a new situation where Zoom[1] or one of its doppelgängers was their only option for connecting with clients and employees.

Virtual work and video conferencing were indeed not unusual, and software like Zoom was making the experience easier. But "not unusual" is not the same as mainstream, and many organizations found a widespread lack of skill in speaking and engaging effectively through the webcam. Some found the transition to be easier than expected, but many struggled on both the organizational and the individual levels. And despite our collective immersion into a virtual communication environment, awkwardness with this medium continues to be a point of stress for many.

We're past the stage where we can blame ineffective virtual communication on a mere lack of experience. In the post-pandemic work economy, virtual communication is now firmly entrenched as an everyday communication option. Yet, even those selfie-taking, Instagramming millennials

---

1. The name Zoom may be used throughout this chapter to refer to any videoconferencing platform, including MS Teams, Skype, Google Meet, etc.

and Gen Z-ers (who seem to have emerged from the womb with smartphones in hand) are susceptible to Zoom fatigue and videoconferencing gaffes. These continued communication struggles can be both confusing and frustrating: how can something so straightforward feel so hard? The promise of virtual communication is that connecting with others is as easy as giving software access to your laptop and webcam. The reality is that virtual is a unique communication environment that requires specific, learned skills and thoughtful, strategic use. To communicate well in this medium, we need to communicate *differently*, adapting subtle behaviors such as gestures and eye contact. We need to communicate *thoughtfully* by making studied choices in how we use this communication tool throughout our workdays.

A Unique Medium for Communication

Communication is strongly affected by the physical and technological environment in which it takes place. The communication environment influences outcomes ranging from our ability to understand one another to whether we find a conversation satisfying or stressful. In-person, telephone, and email conversations all take place in different environments, mediated by differences in the space and/or technology used to have the exchange. Experiences of a conversation can vary considerably even within a certain 'type' of communication environment. Think of the difference between having a work meeting in a cozy café versus a busy, noisy restaurant. These contrasting environments will likely impact your mood, stress levels, and ability to understand the person you're speaking with clearly. The virtual communication environment is cognitively complex, tiring, and often counterintuitive. To communicate well via the webcam, we must understand the unique communication environment created by this medium. Simply put, we can't treat a conversation held via Zoom the same as we would a conversation held in person or over the phone.

One major complication is that videoconferencing is a distraction-heavy environment. Depending on the space we're connecting from, we may be contending with bleeping appliances, ringing doorbells, or intruding children or coworkers. We can be distracted by the physical and virtual backgrounds of other people on the call. We need to contend with staring at our *own* faces during the call, which has a uniquely powerful pull on our attention (Vergallito et al., 2020). And we're doing all this while using devices designed for multitasking. For many of us, it's normal to have several windows, tabs, and apps open at any given time. And we must remember that many apps and programs are deliberately engineered to have addictive elements (Schwär, 2021). Even when we aren't actively using those tabs, the siren call to check our email or social media feed—ever so quickly, of course—is still there.

Basic communication behavior is also different in a virtual environment. When we're sitting in the same room with someone else, we pick up on a host of nonverbal signals. Shrugs, hand gestures, even changes in muscle tension help us understand a bit of what's going on in the other person's head. We make eye contact to show we're listening. We shift eye contact and turn our bodies toward the person we want to speak to next. When we're videoconferencing, however, we often use less nonverbal communication than normal. It's as if the camera has a dampening effect on our physical expressions. We can't pass the conversational baton by looking at or turning our body toward the person who should speak next.

Eye contact—one of the most basic and instinctual communication signals—is especially tricky. Simply put, we can't really make eye contact. For people to feel as though we're looking at them, we need to look into the webcam lens instead of at our screen. Our brains are wired to seek out faces and to read expressions, and overriding our instinct to look at the images of our colleagues on the screen takes a great deal of effort. Most of us end up looking at our screens, not the camera lens, even when we know we "should" have our eyes on the webcam. For cultures that rely on eye contact as a signal that we're paying attention, being in a conversation where everyone appears to be avoiding eye contact can be jarring. And, of course, if we are being mindful to look at our own camera lens, then we can't look at other people's facial expressions ourselves.

When we're on the webcam, we need to use communication behaviors and strategies intended for this environment. The changes aren't difficult or complicated, but they do require us to override communication habits that we've been building our whole lives and be more intentional in our communication choices.

Managing Distractions

Distractions are often a significant issue in all virtual work settings, whether you are in an office, your home, or a remote location. Ideally, people who are engaging in video conferences should have a quiet space to go to, with a lockable door or some sort of "Do Not Disturb" signage. In an office, this could be anything from a dedicated virtual meeting room to a designated quiet area. Home workspaces can be more variable. If you are working in an area that other people have access to, setting up your workspace so that your back is close to a wall can prevent family members from wandering into the camera frame.

An unexpected but significant source of distractions is virtual backgrounds. Whether someone is using a branded company overlay or is simply hiding their room using a "blur background" tool, the effect is the same: strange clipping around their body, choppy movements, and occasional loss of head or limbs if the person moves faster than the program can handle. This is hugely distracting, and the "unreality" of the manipulated background pulls us out of the intimacy of the interaction.

The solution is straightforward: let people see the space you are in. It doesn't need to be glamorous or polished, it just needs to be real and tidy. If that means shoveling scattered toys and laundry to the side so they don't show up in your camera frame, that's fine. What goes on outside your meeting attendees' view doesn't matter. Just be sure to let us see you and the space you're in without the threat of a blur effect chopping your head in half (no beds or bathroom, though—those are locations best left to the imagination).

Even more pressing than visual and environmental distractions is the attention-hogging habit of multitasking during virtual meetings. Our computers and devices, as well as the programs that run on them, are designed to encourage multitasking. Ignoring this siren call is hard, so I recommend relying on software blockers instead of willpower. Blockers such as Strict Pomodoro, Freedom, and Focus all allow you to select what apps and websites you want blocked during your video conference. A quick internet search for "website blockers" will give you many options, though you may need to try a few before finding one that you like. Additional strategies like turning off notifications on your computer and devices and pausing your inbox so that new messages don't come through during your virtual meetings are also helpful.

Optimizing Your Setup

To communicate well on virtual platforms, it's not enough to just turn on our webcam, we need to know how to use it properly. Camera angles, how far away from the camera we sit, and our lighting situation all influence the quality of our interaction. When connecting virtually with clients, stakeholders, and coworkers, we want to re-create the feeling of sitting across the table from one another. We would never have a conversation with a client where we loom over them from on high or have our faces cast in deep, dramatic shadow. Yet, our tech setup often creates these visual effects, and it can be both distracting and off-putting. While fussing over camera angles and position may feel like a vanity project, it's really about making it easier for other people to see your expressions and nonverbal signals. After all, it's hard to see someone gesture when their camera is pointed up their nose.

The first thing to check with your setup is your lighting. Figuring out lighting can be intimidating – it's easy to fall into rabbit holes about soft boxes and ring lights and degrees of Kelvin, but there are only two basic rules to remember:

1. Have plenty of bright, indirect light.

2. Have more light shining on your face than behind you.

With lighting, you want to think like a houseplant: plenty of light, but well diffused so you don't burn your retinas or look washed out. You also need to avoid being backlit, where there is more light shining on the back of your head than on your face (i.e., what happens when sitting with your back to a window). Backlighting will cause your face to disappear into a heavy shadow, making it impossible to see your expressions. If you want to improve your appearance even more, consider having two sources of light, one on either side of your computer at about thirty-degree angles to your face. This will add some feature-enhancing shadows and give your image more depth.

The next setup piece to tackle is your framing: how you appear in the "frame" of the camera when on video. Ideally, you want to be framed so that your body occupies about seven-eighths of the vertical space, with a bit of room between the top of your head and the top of the camera frame. This helps you avoid crowding the camera. You also want to be positioned far enough away from the camera so that people can see you from the middle of your torso to the top of your head. This distancing helps your body language and gestures be more visible.

To avoid awkward angles, such as the dreaded up-the-nose camera view, you will need to ensure your camera lens is at your eye level. You can't rely on just looking at your camera lens or tilting your laptop monitor up or down. You need to raise (or lower) the whole works until the webcam is parallel with your eyeballs while you look straight forward. Minor tilting can help you get the framing right, but it is important that the camera be at the same level as your eyes.

While you generally do not need special equipment to improve your setup, having a good external USB webcam is a great help. The cameras embedded in laptop monitors tend to be poor quality and respond badly to lower light levels. Plus, they're awkward to adjust; you'll need to pile a lot of old textbooks under your laptop to get the right angle. An external webcam, however, is easier to position. A good quality one— which is often available for less than $100—may also have a decent microphone and be able to handle low-light conditions better, making it easier for you to light yourself properly. Smartphone cameras are also excellent. If you rely on a smartphone for your videoconferences, a selfie stick with tripod feet is an excellent tool to have on hand so that you can achieve that perfect camera angle hands-free.

Mindfully Expressive

Nonverbal communication adds important emotional context to our interactions. Facial expressions, gestures, body positioning, and eye contact all contribute to the tone of the conversation and add meaning and context to what we say. Unfortunately, many people tend to use less expression on video than in person, and the camera can't pick up on smaller nonverbal signals. This contributes to the feeling of disconnect that many of us experience in virtual meetings. Our brains are fruitlessly looking for expression and have to backfill much of that missing emotional context, adding to the stress and fatigue of this medium.

Physical expression is a communication behavior that we need to intentionally adapt for videoconferencing. Because nonverbal communication is usually subconscious, it's important to become mindful of our expressions and think about how to use them as part of our overall message. This takes focus and energy, as well as the willingness to get a little uncomfortable and experiment with how you "normally" move or gesture. You'll need to watch yourself on camera, so start a Zoom meeting with yourself and get ready to practice how you mug for the webcam.

The first nonverbal signals to work on are our gestures. Hand and arm gestures bring a great deal of energy to our communication, but they tend to be hidden by our camera framing. Except for the enthusiastic "hands talkers," we spend most of our time gesturing between our hips and mid-chest, which is usually lower than what people can see in a video conference. Getting the framing right by following the recommendations earlier in this chapter will make it easier for people to see our hands.

Once you've adjusted your framing so you're visible from your solar plexus (mid-torso) up, work on moving your hands up so you are regularly gesturing between mid-torso—the bottom of your camera frame—and jaw level. This might be higher than what you're used to. But it's important to get used to having your hands where people can properly see them. Otherwise, all the gesturing in the world is for naught. Avoid gesturing around your head too often, as this can come across as agitated or aggressive.

You are, of course, allowed to drop your hands below your camera frame and relax from time to time. You don't need to be always waving your hands wildly about (nor is that recommended—you don't want to scare the people on your virtual meetings). Just make sure to bring them back up when you want to add energy to your words. A little bit of movement will go a long way, and after a few practice sessions by yourself in a Zoom meeting, you'll get used to gesturing within the camera frame. With a little more practice, it will even start to look and feel natural.

The next nonverbal cue to work on is both the most important and most difficult: to juggle eye contact. Eye contact in virtual meetings is a matter of viewer perception. If you want those you're speaking with to feel as though you're looking at them, you need to look into your webcam lens and *not* at their faces on your monitor. There is no trick to this—you simply need to get used to doing so through practice, repetition, and frequent self-reminders. But there are a few ways to make this habit easier to develop.

First, understand when eye contact is most important. Eye contact in virtual meetings is a strategic action. The times when you want to be deliberate about getting your eyeballs on that camera lens are

- when you're speaking to an issue for more than thirty seconds;

- when you want to place extra emphasis on what

52

you're saying; and

- when other people are speaking, and you want them to feel you're listening closely.

Leveraging eye contact in virtual meetings doesn't mean that you stare relentlessly into the camera lens during the entire conversation. Too much eye contact makes people uncomfortable. It's perfectly fine to look away from the camera, look at the other people on your screen, and give your meeting attendees an "eyeball break" every now and then. Plus, you need to check in with people's facial expressions to get a feel for how the conversation is going. Just think of the camera lens as your home position—one you'll regularly return to. If you find it hard to look at the camera, tape a bull's eye, neon sticky arrows, or something else around the lens so it catches your eyes more easily.

Conversational Flow

Just as virtual communication environments disrupt nonverbal signals, they also muck up the spoken side of things. There are some technical considerations for improving your sound: use a headset (I prefer earbud style) or a USB microphone (many external webcams have decent microphones built in).

Both these options will reduce background noise and echo while improving the overall quality of your sound.

The bigger problem, however, is how virtual affects the flow of conversation. Internet connection lags create micro-delays that throw off the timing of our dialogue. Our inability to use eye contact or body orientation to signal when it's someone's turn leads to awkward pauses and moments where several people try to speak at once. The tendency for certain people to take over the conversation while others retreat into silence is exacerbated. Overcoming these difficulties requires a change in our communication behaviors; namely, we need to stop assuming people will naturally know when to speak and begin deliberately cueing them instead.

Conversation cueing is the simple act of saying the name of the person whose turn it is to speak or to verbally invite people to take part in the conversation. I call this *passing the baton*, as it's much like relay runners handing off the baton to their teammates. Anyone in a virtual meeting can pass a baton, and it's the easiest way to indicate that someone should speak up. While calling on people by name may seem stuffy and prescriptive, in practice, it sounds quite natural:

Bob: "That's the status of the client intake. Lee, is there anything you want to add to this list?"

Lee: "I haven't personally been on any calls with the client this last week, but Kayla mentioned that she was talking with their IT lead yesterday. Kayla, did you discuss anything that should be on this list?"

Kayla: "Yeah, the issues with the forms were resolved, but they've moved on with . . ."

In this little vignette, Bob passed the baton to Lee, who didn't have anything to add but knew Kayla did, so Lee passed the baton to her. People are calling on one another by name and suggesting something specific to speak to. This makes it easier for people to move through the conversation and prevents excessive pauses and pile-on. Keep an eye on people's body language; fidgeting, shifting around, and repeatedly unmuting themselves are all signs that someone wants to speak. People can certainly speak up without being called on—especially if there is a clear opening—but this simple action of cueing people by name smooths out conversations and minimizes how often people speak over one another.

Standards and Schedules: Reducing Virtual Communication Stress

Even with good on-camera communication and savvy conversation management, virtual meetings are a uniquely tiring form of communication. Setting parameters around how and when to use videoconferencing can help prevent Zoom fatigue and burnout. Mindful use of this technology is necessary to make it sustainable in the long run, and organizations wanting to foster healthy, sustainable use of virtual communication platforms should establish and communicate standards of behavior and usage for their employees to follow.

Establishing Etiquette

"Standards of behavior" simply refer to etiquette. Far from being inherently stuffy or prescriptive, etiquette is a shared understanding of how we should behave with one another. It takes the guesswork out of interactions, helping boost professionalism while making people feel more at ease. The purpose of setting organization-wide virtual meeting etiquette is to create a consistent communication experience among all those attending a meeting. You want everyone to show up in the same way. When some people turn up in business button-downs in a neatly appointed home office while others show up in hoodies and are leaning up against bedroom headboards, the tenor of the conversation can be thrown off. Etiquette standards don't need to be stuffy or formal, they just need to be consistent:

Of particular concern is camera etiquette: cameras on or cameras off? Does it even matter? The short answer is, yes, it does. Showing up and interacting on camera takes effort. When some people in a meeting refuse to turn their cameras on, those who are putting in that effort may feel slighted, as though the meeting isn't important enough to those who are off camera to fully participate. It can also make people resentful, as they feel that they're putting more work into the interaction than those hiding behind an empty camera frame. If it goes on too long, this issue of unequal effort can actually eat away at relationships among coworkers.

The issue here isn't whether the cameras *should* be on—sometimes it's a good idea to leave them off, as will be discussed shortly. The important issue is that *everyone does the same thing*. Either everyone's cameras are on, or everyone's cameras are off; that creates a consistent interaction experience that doesn't foster hard feelings. Be sure to clearly communicate whether cameras are to be on or off. This can either be done through policy (i.e., in virtual meetings, cameras are to be turned on unless stated otherwise) or by stating in the meeting invitation whether cameras are to be on or off.

Another point of etiquette is professional appearance. As virtual meetings were suddenly mainstreamed at the start of the pandemic, people who weren't used to virtual and remote work were often confused about the "rules" for how to dress or what parts of their home should be visible on camera. There are no specific rules for what counts as "professional"; it depends on your context. What is considered casual or business-appropriate will vary from organization to organization. It's generally best to set clear guidelines for how people should show up on camera and take away the guesswork. This can reduce a lot of worry about being over- or under-dressed and can prevent other appearance faux pas, such as having questionable artwork in the background or people videoconferencing from their beds.

There are a couple of basic virtual meeting etiquette guidelines that are suitable for every organization. First, what others can see in your camera frame should be neat and tidy. No raunchy posters, no beds in the background. It doesn't need to look like a million-dollar office, but it shouldn't look like a teenager's basement bedroom. Next, establish what counts as acceptable clothing choices. This may reflect your organization's internal culture, the type of work you do, and the expectations of your external clients or stakeholders. You can create categories, such as "casual" (i.e., T-shirts and athleisure), "client-appropriate" (i.e., button-down shirts or company logo wear), or "office formal" (i.e., shirts and suit jackets), to define different styles of dress. If there may be any doubt as to what people should be wearing in a virtual meeting, communicate this in the meeting invitation. For example, an email informing staff of a Zoom meeting with a prospective client could include the line "Cameras on, client-appropriate wear." The etiquette and expectations are now set, and everyone knows exactly how to show up.

There are many other points of virtual meeting etiquette that may be important to establish. Have a discussion with other members of your organization regarding what people consider acceptable behavior in virtual meetings. You may want to set up a "no pets" rule if the parade of cute cats and yapping dogs is overly distracting. Other people may appreciate clarification on whether they can eat while on camera. Discussing virtual meeting behavior and getting agreement on what is appropriate is a useful exercise that can help build organizational culture and team cohesion.

An important note regarding virtual meeting etiquette is about meetings that involve external clients or stakeholders. When meeting with someone from outside your organization, especially if it is a smaller meeting, let the client dictate the etiquette—especially when it comes to cameras on vs. off. If they choose to leave their camera off, don't ask them to turn it on. In fact, it's a good idea to match their approach and turn yours off as well. If you aren't sure whether you should turn yours off, you can simply ask, "Do you mind if I turn my camera off as well?", then act accordingly.

Smart Scheduling

Alongside sorting out standards for etiquette, reducing the amount of time spent on camera can be a big help in reducing Zoom fatigue and communication stress. Not every meeting needs to involve a webcam; phone meetings can provide a nice change of pace, and holding meetings where everyone keeps their cameras off will provide people with a welcome break. Your organization may even want to consider setting one day a week where the entire company commits to having its cameras off. It could be your new casual Friday! When scheduling meetings with people external to your company, offer people a choice—would they prefer to videoconference or have a voice/phone call? If those clients have had it up to their eyeballs with virtual meetings, they may be happy to be given the option of picking up the phone.

In addition to reducing on-camera time, it's important to reduce time spent in meetings overall. It's easy to overdo the number of virtual meetings we agree to—a couple of clicks and our day gets eaten up, block by block. This often leads to people jumping from one meeting to another without the opportunity to mentally process what just happened, never mind getting out of their chair and stretching their legs. Two scheduling tools are useful for putting the brakes on runaway videoconference schedules: transition times and breakout periods.

Implementing thirty-minute transition times between meetings can reduce the mental strain of a day full of Zoom calls. While it may seem inefficient to schedule that much time between meetings, these longer transition times boost productivity and improve alertness. It's common to try leaving ten-minute buffer times between meetings, but this is rarely enough and is frittered away quickly if the meeting runs long. Thirty minutes gives people time to tie up any loose ends for the meeting they just left (make notes, send out promised documents, schedule in follow-ups, and so on), take a short break to get out of their chairs and get comfortable again, and then prep for their next meeting—even if the first meeting runs a few minutes over. The result will be more productive, efficient virtual meetings and less build-up of communication overload throughout the day.

Transition times are useful but aren't enough on their own to prevent virtual meeting burnout. Constant communication is exhausting, and we need periods where we can turn off the communication side of our brains and have longer periods of time for deep thinking work. This is where the practice of setting "blackout periods" becomes useful. Blackout periods are blocks of ninety minutes or longer that appear as "busy" or "unavailable" in our calendars, allowing people to focus on mentally demanding work without the threat of interruption. These periods could be set across an organization or team, or they could be set by individuals, provided both the individual and the people they work with respect the protected time blocks. If you're able to set your own blackout periods, it's a good idea to schedule them according to your own energy levels and work preferences. Some people like to pack all their virtual meetings into a couple of days a week and then give themselves day-long blackout periods, while others prefer doing a few virtual meetings each day and scheduling shorter daily blackout periods. Experiment with different arrangements to find what works for you, and when you set your blackout periods, be sure to respect them. No sneaking in "just one quick meeting!"

Communicating well in a virtual environment takes awareness, effort, and practice. The skills involved in having good virtual meetings are accessible to nearly everyone, but that doesn't make them intuitive or easy. Organizations and workers relying on virtual meetings benefit from engaging thoughtfully with their communication behaviors and choices. From learning how to present oneself well on the webcam to establishing standards of behavior, to creating thoughtful virtual meeting schedules, much goes into the proper use of this important communication tool. The outcomes, however, created by this thoughtful, intentional approach to virtual communication are well worth the effort: more productive conversations, less communication stress, and stronger relationships between clients, coworkers, and stakeholders.

References:

Schwär, H. (2021, August 11). How Instagram and Facebook are intentionally designed to mimic addictive painkillers. *Business Insider.*
https://www.businessinsider.com/facebook-has-been-deliberately-designed-to-mimic-addictive-painkillers-2018-12

Vergallito, A., Mattavelli, G., Gerfo, E. L., Anzani, S., Rovagnati, V., Speciale, M., ... & Lauro, L. J. R. (2020). Explicit and implicit responses of seeing own vs. others' emotions: An electromyographic study on the neurophysiological and cognitive basis of the self-mirroring technique. *Frontiers in Psychology*, 433. https://www.frontiersin.org/articles/10.3389/fpsyg.2020.00433/full?tp=1

Chapter Three

The 4 C's of Developing a Communication Plan to Support Your Virtual Organization

Molly Gutterud

Within the next decade, companies anticipate that more than one-third of their full-time, permanent workforce will work remotely (Inavero 2018). This phenomenon, while accelerated due to the COVID-19 pandemic, was already in motion years before. For communications to be effective, internally and externally, virtual leaders must intentionally foster a culture of autonomy with accountability. As a communications professional, I've seen firsthand how virtual organizations struggle to find effective communication practices, and it can be a challenge to establish a shared culture. To aid in this challenge, I've developed a communication framework based on four C's: culture, content, consistency, and collaboration. This chapter will explore how this communication framework, and a well-defined strategic plan to guide your communication plans, can help virtual organizations communicate more effectively.

Getting Started

A well-rounded communication plan should incorporate constituent insights, feedback loops, assessment plans, and a culture that embraces constructive feedback. The process in which a communication strategy is introduced to an organization can significantly impact the overall process. It is essential to be thoughtful in your choice of words, their impact beyond written text, and the role of executive leadership, middle management, staff, and, ultimately, the intended audience. Gathering insights through surveys and questionnaires from your intended audiences can provide valuable data for making informed decisions and achieving successful outcomes. Listening and acting with their input in mind will build a culture of trust. Without a culture of trust and transparency, the reliability of the data may be compromised, making launching an effective communication plan more difficult.

In a recent podcast, Brené Brown (2022) challenged the notion of creating a safe environment, stating that safety isn't achieved simply by saying so. Instead, one can foster a brave space for encouraging dissenting opinions and promoting continuous improvement. For this part, language matters. Inclusive language and partnering with Diversity, Equity, and Inclusion (DEI) professionals are essential for effective communications, especially in today's diverse and interconnected world.

A well-structured communications plan enables an organization to convey its strategies and objectives clearly and consistently, enhancing brand identity, internal and external relationships, and overall business outcomes. The principles that define organizational strategic planning are applicable to building communications plans. According to Wolf and Floyd (2017), strategic planning includes defining organizational goals, strategies, and programs designed to achieve objectives through successfully implementing policies and procedures. Every organization should have a strategic plan that's aligned with the organization's mission, vision, and values. Strategic planning is an organization's North Star, helping ensure all staff and leaders are working toward achieving the same goals. Effective communication plans are key to following the organization's identified North Star, and communication plans should be developed following strategic plan guidelines and principles. Following this strategy will build awareness, garner support, and foster trust through communications.

Constituent Insights

Collecting constituent insights through surveys and questionnaires allows your constituents to inform the strategy, and provides an opportunity to receive input from diverse perspectives. In this initial planning stage, establishing benchmarks for your organization's current communication practices allows for a better understanding of constituent needs and the current cultural climate of the organization. Utilizing surveys and questionnaires to gather data regarding the most critical topics, preferred communication methods, and desired frequency provides you with the building blocks for the foundation to develop the next phase of the communication plan. Using data to inform your strategy is a sustainable and measurable approach that keeps your constituents' needs in mind as you move forward.

Feedback Loops

Establishing ongoing feedback channels is crucial for a communication plan to be effective. The goal of using a feedback loop is to develop a system that allows you to learn and evolve as you go. Industries evolve rapidly, and global economics are changing at an unprecedented pace. By keeping open lines of communication, you can remain flexible and prepared to respond to unexpected events. An example of a feedback loop is an anonymous survey shared with constituents. This provides a secure and accessible channel to receive honest and transparent feedback anytime. This could also be achieved by creating an email alias for staff to send questions or feedback directly.

The most critical component to consider is your action once you receive feedback. Encourage and celebrate input, and have leaders share examples of submissions that contribute to the strategic direction. This process fosters trust within the organization. It demonstrates to the people within the organization that feedback and participation are appreciated. It is essential to clarify that asking for participation doesn't guarantee that every suggestion will be implemented. However, it's necessary to acknowledge that you are actively listening and value the insights shared. By providing opportunities for individuals to contribute their perspectives, you can bring the organization closer to its mission and foster a sense of involvement and ownership.

Assessment and Learning

Develop a plan for measuring success and communicate it to internal and external constituents. Clearly define your approach and commit to it. You do not need all the answers or data to establish how success is measured within your organization. Ensure that your assessment measures align with your mission and vision, with a clear commitment to your constituents.

Strategic plans have a reputation for being a multi-year strategy that ultimately collects dust on a shelf and is only taken down to review when it's coming to the final year. Strategic plans should be dynamic and adaptable to the ever-changing impacts of the industry, social influences, and world economies. Incorporating intentional organizational assessments periodically throughout the strategic plan allows you to identify areas for adjustment as needed and hold the organization accountable.

The Four Cs of Communicating: Culture, Consistency, Collaboration, Content

In this section, you are introduced to the four Cs of communicating. After considering what is outlined above in preparation for developing a communication strategy aligned with your strategic plan, it's time to use the data to inform the development of the actual communication. Use the following prompts in these sections to develop a comprehensive and culturally responsive communication plan.

Culture

Schein (1990) defined *culture* as a widely held, shared set of values, beliefs, and ideas. These three culture attributes are the core that defines an organization. In a virtual organization, it's essential to establish a strong culture that can guide decision-making and help team members feel connected to one another. To better understand your organization's cultural landscape, consider posing these questions to your members:

- How does the past inform your future?

- How is your organization committed to modeling effective organizational behaviors?

- What is the industry's environmental landscape?

- How will you meet the challenges ahead?

To cultivate a strong culture within a virtual organization, consider implementing these strategies:

- Develop a mission statement: A mission statement can help team members understand the organization's goals and what it stands for.

- Encourage regular communication: Virtual team members can feel isolated, so it's essential to encourage frequent communication through video calls, instant messaging, and email.

- Establish core values: Identifying and communicating core values can help team members feel a sense of belonging and shared purpose.

- Promote a diverse and inclusive culture: Using inclusive language and partnering with DEI professionals can help promote a culture of DEI in an organization. This can foster an environment where varying ideas are welcome, employees feel a sense of belonging and increase creativity and innovation.

Consistency

Consistency is fundamental to building trust and credibility in a virtual organization. It is essential to maintain consistent communication across all channels and ensure that team members receive the same information. Pay careful attention to your audiences and tailor your messages accordingly. By consistently delivering accurate and precise communication, you become a trusted source of information that helps foster a sense of cohesion within the organization. Warrell (2012) discussed that the risks of communicating from a distance consist of the probability of mistrust, coldness, and lack of empathy. Be sure to evaluate your consistency regarding whom you inform, what information you share, and when you communicate. Consider the social and emotional impacts of the topics you address and how they may affect different members of your organization. Establishing robust policies and procedures that align with current practices will allow you to maintain consistency across various communication needs.

Although the task of documenting current practices may appear daunting, it serves as a highly effective method for creating well-considered processes and making them accessible to organization members. Creating a standard communication policy for your organization will ensure consistency and efficacy, particularly during challenging moments. Though often seen as tedious, these policies and procedures are essential. Documenting policies and procedures provide clear guidelines for crisis communication, ensuring that chaos does not disrupt the function of your organization and allows issues to be addressed swiftly and gracefully.

To maintain consistency, incorporate these key elements into every communication strategy:

- Audience: Internal – staff, leadership, partner organizations, and board members. External – customers, regulatory agencies, accrediting bodies.

- Modality: Leveraging technology can be effective, but sometimes too much can be a distraction. Be intentional in your choice of delivering news and the technology used. Virtual town halls, email, text messaging, organization intranet, newsletters, and social media are great tools if leveraged consistently (don't forget to measure this performance and effectiveness continuously).

Not everyone consumes information in the same way. So, how do you meet the needs of your varying audiences? Choose a path using data collected from your constituent surveys. That data can help inform when and how to best communicate important information to your organization.

Effective communication plans use multiple modes of communication launched strategically to ensure the information received and expectations are clearly explained to the intended audience (Young et al., 2019). Consider these strategies to promote consistency as you develop your communication plans:

- Use a centralized communication platform: A centralized platform like Slack or Microsoft Teams can help ensure everyone can access the same information.

- Create communication guidelines: Guidelines help ensure that communication is consistent in tone, style, and format.

- Provide regular updates: Regular updates can help team members stay informed and prevent confusion. I cannot stress enough how important it is to be intentional about the frequency of communication. Ask yourself if you are trying to be quick or thoughtful in responding; sometimes slower is faster.

The strategies above rely heavily on technology and organizational infrastructure. What is the current state of your organization's technological infrastructure? Is it a pain point or an asset? Do you have the technology to support the modality and measure it effectively? Harpool (2020) stated that it is imperative to differentiate between moving in-person educational courses online and having the infrastructure to offer distance-based learning effectively. It would be best to have an established infrastructure (including technology) to create a sustainable and effective virtual organization. The same principles apply when developing a strategic communication plan for a virtual or hybrid organization.

Collaboration

Collaboration is essential in a virtual organization, where team members may work on different aspects of a project. To better understand and facilitate collaboration, it can be divided into three categories: planning, execution, and evaluation. Collaborative planning, execution, and evaluation facilitate alignment with project goals, foster smooth implementation, and yield valuable insights for ongoing organizational improvement and success.

The first category, planning, must be an inclusive process that involves all relevant internal leaders. Identify your key leadership stakeholders and ensure they are included in the planning, execution, and evaluation process. This will help with data accuracy and alignment within the organization.

Collaboration at all levels shows that an organization values and respects all people, which can create a positive reputation and increase customer loyalty. Inclusive language and partnering with a DEI professional are essential to effective communications. They can promote a diverse and inclusive culture, build trust and credibility, avoid unintended offenses, enhance accessibility, and ensure legal compliance. Organizations can improve communications and create positive relationships with their audiences by prioritizing inclusive language with DEI.

The second category, execution of a communication plan, must begin with conveying the information from the top down following a scaffolded approach. Information is first communicated from executive leadership, senior leadership, and middle management. This allows the organization's leaders to consume the information, consider impacts on their teams, inform needs for training, and provide insights into the potential questions or concerns that might arise. In organization-wide communication surveys I've conducted, I've asked two questions: What information is most valuable to you, and how do you prefer to receive the information? The top responses from team members included "information necessary to do my job" and "I prefer to receive information from my direct leader or supervisor." Using these data, the scaffolded approach allows leadership to establish a message and consistent understanding. Hence, all audiences receive the same information from someone they know and trust. As information is communicated to the broader organization, leaders are prepared for follow-up questions which helps foster trust, clarity, and a healthy culture.

The third category, evaluation, includes measuring the effectiveness of your organization's predetermined metrics before launching the plan. This can consist of engagement analytics, additional feedback surveys, and existing or new technology to help inform the organization where investments should be made. Refrain from being so focused on what lies ahead that you forget to reflect on how you did. Invite stakeholders back to the conversation to see learning and continuous improvement. With more collaboration comes understanding and aligned commitment to more effective means of execution. Consider the following strategies to promote collaboration:

- Use project management tools: Project management tools like Trello or Asana can help team members stay organized and collaborate more effectively.

- Encourage teamwork: Promoting teamwork and regular check-ins can help team members work together toward common goals.

- Foster a culture of feedback: Create an environment

where team members are encouraged to give and receive feedback to identify and resolve issues quickly.

Content

Content is the information that an organization communicates to its team members and external stakeholders. In a virtual organization, it's essential to ensure that content is clear, concise, and engaging. Partnering with DEI professionals means working with experts who promote diversity, equity, and inclusion in organizations throughout the entire planning and execution process. Ensure the organization has a policy for respectful and inclusive language for all people regardless of gender, race, ethnicity, sexual orientation, religion, or ability. This includes ensuring that communication is accessible to people with disabilities. Establish a writing style guide for your organization to provide consistency with messaging from your organization. Style guides should include guidelines for the following content:

Multimodal Communications

- Email

- Intranet

- Social media

- Newsletters

Policies

- Communication standards

- Social media policy

- Media relations policy

Intake, Development, Approvals, Deployment

- Requests: intake process

- Reviews: review process

- Approvals: approval process

- Deployment: delivery of communication

Writing Style Guidelines

- Names and proper nouns/titles

- Signature block

- Abbreviations and acronyms

- Punctuation, pronouns, age

- Fonts, colors, branding

Consider the following strategies to create compelling content:

- Use visuals: Visuals like infographics and videos can be more engaging than text alone.

- Keep it simple: Use precise language and avoid jargon or technical terms that may not be familiar to everyone.

- Tailor your message: Different team members may have different information needs, so it's essential to tailor your message to your audience.

- Internal and external alignment: External marketing and media should be aligned with internal messaging for consistency and clarity for the consumer and internal staff.

Utilizing inclusive language and collaborating with DEI professionals are crucial steps in guaranteeing that your content accurately conveys its intended message while fostering a diverse and inclusive environment. Here are some guidelines to follow:

- Using inclusive language by intentionally speaking

to the audience creates trust and credibility and a space where they can feel safe, seen, and heard.

- Avoid unintended offense by avoiding non-inclusive language or imagery. Whether intentional or not, words can offend or alienate audiences. This can lead to negative consequences, including lost business, negative publicity, and legal challenges.

- Inclusive language can improve accessibility by using clear and concise language and avoiding jargon and acronyms to make communication more accessible. In addition, ensure that images in communications have the alternate text available for screen readers and videos have closed captioning included.

Conclusion

Effective communication is essential for virtual organizations to succeed. Notice how DEI was mentioned throughout the chapter. DEI should not be a stand-alone component of a strategic plan or communication strategy. It must be intentionally integrated throughout the entire process; it is a lens the organization uses to help inform strategic direction and as a learning opportunity. Ensuring DEI is part of the organization's value system is not the job of a single individual or team; all members within an organization should feel ownership and responsibility to provide feedback and participate with an equity-focused mindset. Strategic planning and effective communication go hand in hand when introducing new initiatives or organizational changes that impact your entire community.

You are responsible for driving your organization forward to be successful and sustainable. Organizations can establish a strong culture, promote consistency, foster collaboration, and create compelling content by using the four Cs framework of culture, consistency, collaboration, and content. By successfully implementing these strategies, virtual organizations can communicate more effectively and achieve strategic goals without the need for team members to be in a shared physical space. Regardless of where members of an organization are physically located, the strength and success of an organization can be realized through trust, action, and clear, concise communication.

References

Brown, B. (Host). (2022, November 17). Building brave spaces [Audio podcast episode]. In *Dare to Lead with Brené Brown*. https://brenebrown.com/podcast/building-brave-spaces/

Harpool, D. (2020, April 20). Online classes a necessity now, but they're not true online learning. *Times of San Diego*. https://timesofsandiego.com/opinion/2020/04/20/online-classes-a-necessity-now-but-theyre-not-true-online-learning/

Inavero. (2018, February 26). 2018 future workforce report: Hiring manager insights on flexible and remote work trends. https://www.slideshare.net/upwork/2018-future-workforce-report-hiring-manager-insights-on-flexible-and-remote-work-trends

Schein, E. H. (1990). Organizational culture. *American Psychologist*, 45, 109-119.

Warrell, M. (2012, August 27). Hiding behind email? Four times you should never use email. *Forbes.* *https://www. Forbes.com/sites/margiewarrell/2012/08/27/do-you-hidebehind-*email/#392978e8238c

Wolf, C., & Floyd, S. W. (2017). Strategic planning research: Toward a theory-driven agenda. *Journal of Management 43*(6), 1754-1788. https://doi.org/10.1177/0149206313478185

Young, C., DeMarco, C., Nyysti, K., Harpool, A., & Mendez T. (2019). The role of faculty development in online universities. In K. Walters & P. Henry (Eds.) *Fostering Multiple Levels of Engagement in Higher Education Environments*, (pp.

268–268). IGI Global. DOI: 10.4018/978-1-5225-7470-5.
ch012

Section III – Engagement

Engagement

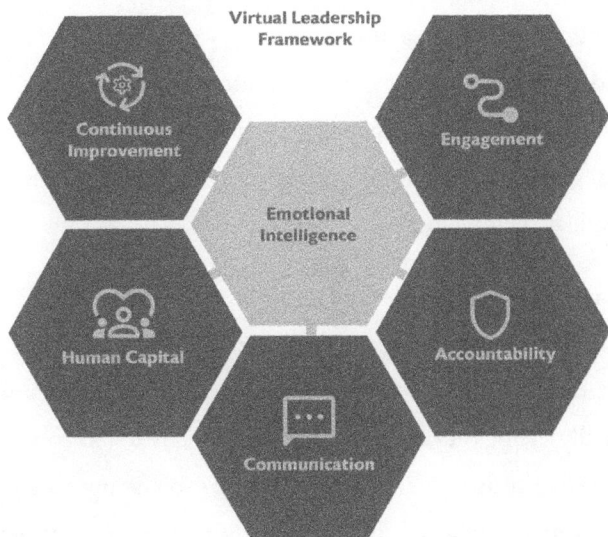

Virtual Leadership Framework

Continuous Improvement

Engagement

Emotional Intelligence

Human Capital

Accountability

Communication

Chapter Four

The Power of Leading Remotely

Elizabeth Kemp Caulder

W orking virtually is an employee-centric approach. It provides much-needed flexibility for our team members, leading to a more enriching work experience that yields increased quality, higher productivity, and reduced turnover rates. Many organizations have learned some key strategies to make remote work a reality that works for them as well as their teams.

Despite a quarter of executives in Future Forum's (2022) recent survey indicating their culture is being negatively impacted by offering flexible work policies, flexible workers are actually saying they are as likely or more likely to feel connected to their teams, their managers, and the company's values. In an interesting article in *Harvard Business Review* that analyzed meeting trends from 2020 to 2022, Brodsky and Tolliver (2022) shared findings that indicated workers did not seem to have become less engaged, but more engaged.

Once upon a time, when people would talk about "remote employees," one would immediately envision colleagues who had little to no meaningful ties to the organization and had no connection to the organization's culture, working alone in a sad, drab office space in some distant location. That reality has changed, thanks to advances in technology that have shifted not just how we connect at work but how we connect in play. Today, remote work is a convenient, productive option for both the employee and the company. Yes, remote work is employee-centric, but it is company-centric, as well. In addition to the flexibility that it provides our team members, it also allows our organizations to tap into talent outside of our commuter geography of our brick-and-mortar offices. We can now employ the best people, wherever they may be, which makes us more diverse in thought, experience, and perspective, and makes us more competitive.

Forgive my soap-box diatribe, but I spent many years working in leadership at an organization that refused to even consider testing remote work for leadership roles. This adamant decision was despite several structural truths that would have made remote work not just logical but a solution to the growing problems within the organization. The first was the requirement for middle and upper management to travel extensively across the country. You might ask why the ownership would be so unwilling to allow its leaders, who were often on the road and working remotely anyway, to live and work from a place other than in the vicinity of the brick-and-mortar headquarters (HQ). I asked the question quite often (and perhaps even more than they would have preferred), especially when this decision significantly reduced the potential talent pool for open leadership positions. It was incredibly limiting.

❧ ⋅ ✦ ⋅ ❧

As brand strategists by trade, my team and I are often leading organizations through in-depth, strategic brand planning to drive organizational growth. One of the universal truths that we impart to our clients in the facilitation of these brand development or brand refinement sessions is that a company's internal marketing is just as important—and I would argue even more important—than external marketing initiatives. In this way, companies are defined by the culture they create.

I am a firm believer that, as a leader, it's important to understand that culture impacts your team members' personal engagement as well as the collective productivity of your team.

At the end of the day, the best success metric is to constantly gauge and understand the answers to two questions:

Number One: Are your team members happy?

Number Two: Regardless of whether the answer to the first question is yes or no, what else can we do within our power to enhance the experience of our team to demonstrate their value to our firm?

A good example of this in action is the reason why I founded The Phoenix on the promise and premise of remote work and a commitment to prioritizing life in "life/work balance." Suffice it to say that company culture was an integral component of the planning stage for my agency.

I want to ensure that my team of creatives can work from wherever they are happiest and most fulfilled, with a level of flexibility that allows people to schedule their lives and work in ways that are harmonious on an individual level. I am also intentional about building upon healthy, diverse, inclusive cultural aspects that are regularly evaluated and updated to become optimized. I want to ensure that each and every day our team members are completely comfortable showing up as their truest selves and know, without question, they belong and are valued. In the face of labor shortages, inflation, and discussions around a potential economic depression, organizational leadership teams are now coming to realize that if they want to retain the people they have selected and invested valuable time and resources in training and developing, they will need to be willing to compromise and be prepared to provide more flexibility.

Still, it is understandable that those who have not figured out the secret to effectively leading a remote workplace may be having a difficult time navigating this new way of operating their businesses and their teams. Whether it be the multitudes of individual workers still challenged by the transition to their remote work routine, the managers struggling with leading their remote teams, or the droves of people who are hoping and praying that their employers do not force them back into a brick-and-mortar office, the topic of working remotely seems to be on everyone's minds.

Having this amazing opportunity to lead a company full of gifted brand strategists, designers, and support specialists working remotely across North and South America (after nearly three decades spent in the leadership of an organization that required physical presence in the office) has been quite refreshing. I have long believed that where people get their work done shouldn't matter if they are working hard and de-livering every day. Affording your team the flexibility to work where and when they need to be is not just employee-centric, it's company-centric, as well. Our remote model allows our team members to achieve a much better life/work (intentionally flipped) balance, increases their commitment to the company, and maximizes their productivity. The resulting motivation yields creativity and innovation that assures the highest quality work product is produced each and every day. This is why I founded Phoenix Lifestyle Marketing Group, predicated on the unwavering commitment to remote work.

Nonetheless, I must admit that running a company powered by remote work is not without its challenges. Here are my five tips to help organizational leaders effectively wield the power of leading remotely that can help teams to remain productive as we charge forth into the evolution of how organizations operate. T.E.A.M.S. is an acronym that I use to help keep these tips top of mind.

T Is for TRUST

Trusting your team members and ensuring that they can trust and rely on one another is paramount. If you can't trust your employees to work remotely, why hire them in the first place? I have heard so many horror stories about the lack of trust in people who are working remotely. Keystroke monitoring by leadership, managers assessing calendars, workers concerned about running out to the store to grab food and supplies for their families during the "workday." Seriously, folks? Please allow your employees to set their own schedules within clearly outlined parameters so that they can efficiently and effectively complete their work while balancing their other priorities.

E Is for ENGAGE

Engaging consistently and transparently is paramount to ensuring that your team members feel that they are part of a larger whole, and that they can trust you, as well. Making certain that you keep your remote team members in the loop so that they do not feel like they are on an island alone can be a unique challenge. Keeping everyone informed is as much about timing and delivery as it is about transparency and clarity. Without a well-developed communication strategy, even sharing an exciting update haphazardly, could be detrimental to morale. As a leader, you also have a responsibility to create an environment that fosters regular two-way communication. This is not limited to project status meetings but should also include making the scheduling of one-to-one check-ins the norm. I am intentional about regular water-cooler convos with my team members, understanding that without the traditional in-office dynamic, we won't run into one another in the hallway or on the way to lunch. Therefore, it is very important to ensure that those informal chats actually occur regularly in the remote workplace.

I also keep an open-door policy to ensure that my team feels comfortable reaching out to me with questions or thoughts, whether work-related or not. Although checking in is a really great way to ensure that your team members feel seen and valued, I am a firm believer that engagement through acknowledgment and celebrations makes a considerable impact, as well. Providing intentional, constructive feedback on projects and recognition of a job well done can go a long way. We also do a great job of celebrating special dates, birthdays, holidays, and anniversaries together, which also lets our folks know that they are valued and appreciated and part of our "Phoenix Phamily."

A Is for AVOID

I think it is critical that leaders avoid unnecessary interruptions of their team members' days. I recall a time in my career when a fellow member of the leadership team would regularly announce people's names over the office-wide intercom system to report to his office. This type of interruption was detrimental to morale because it implied that whatever those employees were working on was less important than whatever question or topic was driving the need for this impromptu meeting.

All the productivity that results from remote work can be undermined by an unscheduled non-emergency phone/video call. It also can inadvertently communicate a lack of importance for that activity in which the team members may be currently engaged. I make it a point to encourage my team to use their calendars to update their availability. It's important also to make it clear that they do not just include their business meetings and projects, but also their personal needs, such as lunch, doctor's appointments, school check-ins, self-care activities, etc. This will help you to identify when to reach out to your team member and when to leave them to it!

M Is for MAKE USE

Making good use of technology and tools is critical to leading remote teams. Fortunately, there continues to be new tools developed, and people are using them both for work and for personal entertainment, so technological integration and evolution should be expected. Remember that video conferencing and project management tools are your friends. These tools not only help to streamline work, but they also can be great mediums to help you collaborate on projects and stay connected with your team members. We use our preferred platform as a great tool to achieve all the above. At The Phoenix, we are committed to enabling video during virtual meetings. Especially with remote work, body language and eye contact are important components of communication. Our team also makes it a point to begin and end our meetings by sharing anecdotes or general chit-chat.

It's also important to avoid making the mistake of relegating your use of video conferencing or chats to just project or company updates. These tools present a prime opportunity to connect meaningfully with remote team members about all types of work and non-work-related topics. Find time for small talk! You can use the time to get to know your team as individuals and to gain perspective on how things are going. Allowing them to share more about themselves or even asking for their opinions on your processes and procedures helps build a better relationship between them and the company. Remember, when there are no water-cooler or lunchroom conversations, it is necessary to actively make intentional connections.

S Is for SCHEDULE

When you're working off a calendar, it is incredibly important that you do not miss the opportunity to schedule some fun. I mean, let's face it, "all work and no play" isn't a good mantra for any company culture. As organizations and leaders struggle to lead remote teams while maintaining focus on project timelines, revenue growth, and the like, it's pretty easy to get lost in a sea of status meetings, client conference calls, and project workstreams. One thing to keep in mind is that the silly conversations and funny episodes that happen in the hallways of a brick-and-mortar setting are an integral part of the way that meaningful, emotional connections are made among a team.

Although it is necessary to set clear expectations for work projects, it is equally important to remember to ensure that your team remains connected on a personal level and you remain connected to each of them too. Team happy hours, surprise and delight activities, and team game days are a great way to keep your team engaged. Let loose and have some fun!

I am often asked where my passion for advocating for the value of virtual organizations, and my commitment to optimizing how to lead remotely, began. It is very hard to pinpoint. At this point in my career, I feel like "forever" seems like a pretty accurate copout, but an evasion, nonetheless. Thinking back, not to B-School, but rather to the days of my undergraduate studies, I have fond memories of a professor who started the semester on the very first day of class freshman year by proclaiming that he would not be taking attendance. He said that as long as we returned to take the final exam, we could complete the course as we wished. That was definitely an attention grabber, even prompting a few students to turn right back around and walk out the doors of the lecture hall. The professor also said something that has had a profound impact on my approach to management and my personal leadership style. He said something like, "Attendance is merely a powerplay between professor and student to demonstrate that the professor has control over the actions and the whereabouts of the student and has absolutely nothing to do with the student's ability to learn or the professor's ability to impart wisdom to the student. This powerplay is a game in which I have no desire to engage." The professor explained that for this reason, he had no attendance policy.

Despite the lack of attendance policy, he did make certain that we knew that he would be in the lecture hall every Monday, Wednesday, and Friday at 8 a.m., lecturing on the material that the class syllabus indicated should be covered at that point in the semester. He also assured us that he would be on-site to engage in discussion and answer any questions that we may have related to the reading or the work outlined in the class curriculum. Nonetheless, he assured us that he would not take attendance and he would therefore not be penalizing students (or rewarding them) based on their decision to show up for, or skip, his lectures.

This was a departure from the norm for most students, many of us emerging from our high-school shells. We were used to a routine for tracking and rewarding us for simply showing up in the designated location. The professor informed us that, as adults, we should be responsible to manage our commitment to learning. He explained that it was neither his responsibility nor his right to micromanage that process for us. Though excited about the thought of not having to get up and trudge across a blistery cold campus in Upstate New York, I was also intrigued by the idea of self-navigating my learning journey—excited about the flexibility it offered, and comfortable with the personal accountability that was required.

Although our professor was clear that he truly wanted us to be successful, he was also clear that he trusted us to manage our time, prioritize tasks, and complete work as necessary to achieve a successful outcome. I remember him telling us that if we could be successful without having to be physically present, why should he or anyone else have a problem with that?

That particular experience was very powerful to me. I bet that professor would be surprised how this has remained with me for the past thirty years since; and it has interestingly become an important part of my journey to remote leadership throughout my career. That experience has shaped my remote leadership philosophy and continues to support the pillars of how we lead and inspire new leaders—Trust, Communicate, Support, Evaluate—at my agency, The Phoenix Lifestyle Marketing Group.

The very first, and most important, pillar is Trust. I am a firm believer that in leadership, regardless of whether remote, hybrid, or otherwise, it is imperative to trust your team to do the job that they were hired to do. After all, in addition to the fact that we are talking about adults, these people are professionals who were carefully recruited and selected based on their special skills and experience. And, let's face it, if leaders are micromanaging others, how are they leading the organization or their division? How are they building and strengthening their teams? And let us not venture down the path of what happens when there is a lack of trust.

I'd also argue that the other pillars (Communicate, Support, and Evaluate) are also applicable regardless of whether the role is remote: Communicate the clear expectations that have been set to ensure they know the pathway to, and the picture of, success (which relates to evaluation). Then be sure to provide consistent, accessible support so that your team can engage along the way.

It's important that your teams know that support and guidance are there for them when they need it. This brings reassurance. For those who feel more comfortable with direct, ongoing support, encouragement, and direction, establishing open access to ensure that their developmental needs are being met will ensure that they feel supported and well-positioned for success.

References

Brodsky, A., & Tolliver, M. (2022, December 6). No, remote employees aren't becoming less engaged. *Harvard Business Review*. https://hbr.org/2022/12/no-remote-employee s-arent-becoming-less-engaged

Future Forum. (2022, October). Future forum pulse: Executives feel the strain of leading in the "new normal." https://futureforum.com/research/pulse-report-fall -2022-executives-feel-strain-leading-in-new-normal

Chapter Five

Engaging Hybrid Employees by Leveraging the Magic of Recognition

Geraldine Woloch-Addamine

"The world is constantly changing" was always the first sentence by one of my favorite leaders when announcing corporate reorganizations. Usually, a silence was followed by a long pause, allowing me to prepare for the worst. It was a brilliant way to prepare her audience for difficult conversations.

Since the 2020 pandemic, change is everywhere, and resilience has become a strategic core value. The future of work has been spared five or ten years of micro changes in a giant leap of technological acceleration, with artificial intelligence (AI) at the forefront of everything.

Currently, we're discussing a "confusing economy" where new trends might be temporary, and earlier debates over hiring in the tech industry have evolved into ugly, massive layoffs two years later. These economic paradoxes of high inflation, low unemployment, and sustained productivity hide a global constant: the employee engagement rate has deteriorated worldwide. People feel less belonging and greater disconnect in the workplace under the stressors of the pandemic and the challenges of hybrid work communications.

So, where can we begin with employee engagement?

Recognition: Where We Begin in the Quest for Engaging Employees in the Hybrid Workplace

Tensions in the workplace keep growing due to rising individualism and social polarization. It's urgent to rethink performance through individual recognition to help people feel valued and appreciated. Recognition can also relate to the perception of fairness—a driver of performance and retention at work—highly expected by new generations.

Let's dig in and start with a quick assessment of our current workforce.

Workforce Disengagement

For the first time, we have the four generations working together simultaneously:

1. Baby boomers (1946–1964): 25.5% of the US workforce

2. Gen X (1965–1980): 43.7% of the US workforce

3. Millennials (1981–2000): 39.8% of the US workforce

4. Gen Z (2000–present): 10% of the US workforce[1]

We can experience a lot of communication frustrations in the workplace due to generational issues.

---

1. Note that the percentages do not add up due to generational overlaps. (U.S. Bureau of Labor Statistics, 2023)

In terms of disengagement, we also face some disparities among generations. According to the 2022 *State of the Global Workplace,* only 15% of employees feel engaged. Overall, people don't feel an emotional connection to their work and mostly do what's expected. The burnout of at least a third of the US workforce—continually reported since 2020—is not a specific millennial phenomenon. Instead, it accelerated with the adoption of remote or hybrid working and the flexibility request for well-being. Now, the expectation of a better work/life balance is intergenerational (Gallup, 2022).

As with the expectation of more fairness and respect in the workplace, tough talks on social issues are more accepted because of the momentum gained after the tragic death of George Floyd in 2020. Other factors include the opening of the global talent pool, normalizing remote work, and nomad workers, all of which have created a more diverse workforce.

While the rise of individualism risks inhibiting collective performance, it fuels growing expectations for more respect and fairness to mitigate opposite views in the workplace. Strengthening good relationships becomes critical for people to work together effectively.

From the great resignation phenomenon to the great retention, we have devolved into the great disconnection and the disengagement horror movie.

Employee Recognition, Trust, and Engagement in the Hybrid Workplace

In France, when you recognize a team member, you invite them to a private lunch in a good restaurant for at least one or two hours. You have time to build relationships and create trust. In the US, you celebrate a performance through public praise. You become the employee of the month and win an award. You want to showcase your prize on your office desk to build a "visible" reputation that fosters credibility and trust.

The Magic of Recognition

Indeed, in private or public recognition, cultural differences are important to consider in celebrating people's performance. Yet, recognition remains the best way to motivate employees, with a proven direct correlation with employee engagement. Research from Quantum Workplace (2023) shows that employees are 2.7 times more likely to be highly engaged when they believe they will be recognized.

Recognition increases productivity by creating a positive work environment for cooperation. It fosters a trusting culture that allows people to stay longer with the company. When you look at Maslow's hierarchy of needs, the magic of recognition hits all five levels of human needs: survival, security, belonging, importance, and self-actualization.

There's a neuroscientific explanation behind the power of recognizing people. Paul J. Zak (2017) explains the phenomenon in his book *Trust Factor: How Recognition and Praise Release Oxytocin*. The human body releases a brain chemical that contributes to a sense of safety, security, and peace, helping us process strong emotions like stress. Oxytocin contributes to reducing burnout, building trust, and strengthening relationships—it fuels that feeling of belonging we need, as a highly social species, to face threats. And it might be the best medicine to reduce stress in the hybrid workplace.

After the pandemic, people became more stressed at work than ever. In the hybrid workplace, it's worth investing in employee recognition programs. Employee well-being has become a significant concern and a global trend. Moreover, survival and the quest for security have pushed people to turn inward. No wonder that increased focus on survival has also fostered a rise in individualism. That in turn promotes powerful identity assertions, with increased conflicts and tensions in the hybrid workplace.

To best support people and move them toward the security level of the Maslow pyramid, they must feel safe, respected, and engaged through recognition programs. Against this backdrop, the employee recognition market will grow, with a forecast of a 13.4% growth to reach USD 34.1 billion by 2030, according to Acumen Research and Consulting (2023).

We have also observed the rise of the gig economy, with more short-term contracts in many countries. But across generations, whether employee tenure is longer or shorter, the stake for performance and productivity is the same: it's all about focusing on engaging employees more than retaining them.

In the ever-changing workplace driven by technology, leadership will always have access to one magic wand for increasing employee engagement and satisfaction: people recognition.

References

Acumen Research and Consulting. (2023, January 3). Employee recognition system market size set to achieve USD 34.1 billion by 2030 growing at 13.4% CAGR. *Global Newswire.* https://www.globenewswire.com/news-release/2023/01/03/2582036/0/en/Employee-Recognition-System-Market-Size-Set-to-Achieve-USD-34-1-Billion-by-2030-growing-at-13-4-CAGR-Exclusive-Report-by-Acumen-Research-and-Consulting.html

Gallup. (2022). *State of the global workplace: 2022 report.* https://www.gallup.com/workplace/349484/state-of-the-gl

obal-workplace.aspx?utm_source=google&utm_medium=c
pc&utm_campaign=california_gallup_access_branded&ut
m_term=gallup%20engagement%20survey&gclid=Cj0KC
QiAxbefBhDfARIsAL4XLRrmDNL7uwI15FZD3nAQT
Gbz2DiLB9Y2rzY9g_EnXHPKa9XwkNKOgDAaAuEDE
ALw_wcB#ite-393248

Quantum Workplace (2023). *The importance
of employee recognition: Statistics and research*. https://www.quantumworkplace.com/future-of-wo
rk/importance-of-employee-recognition

U.S. Bureau of Labor Statistics. (2023). *Labor force participation rates in 1992, 2002, 2012, and projected 2022, by age*.
Chart Data. https://www.bls.gov/opub/ted/2014/ted_201
40106.htm

Zak P.J. (2017). *Trust Factor: The science of creating high-per-
formance companies*. AMACOM.

Section IV – Accountability

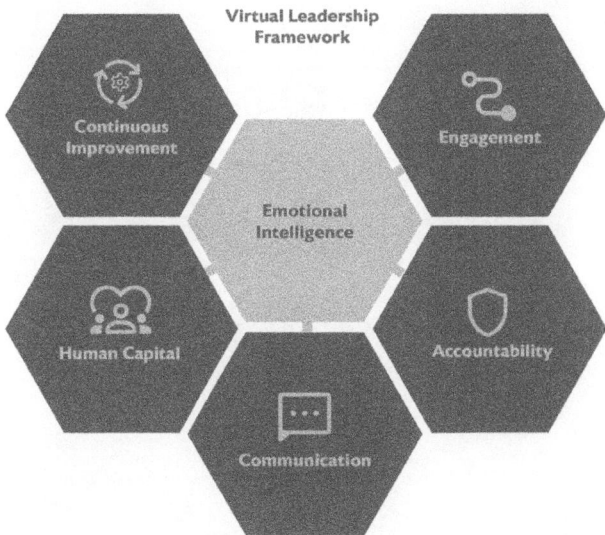

Chapter Six

Creating a Culture of Accountability in a Remote and Hybrid World

Anand Madhavan

The Story of Accountability

Accountability, by and large, changed dramatically during COVID, and continues now as we enter a post-pandemic (or endemic) world. To understand how different things were, and to understand where we are now, we need to first define what accountability is. Then, we need to understand how employees and managers view accountability, and why we might have missed the mark when we think about overall organizational culture.

Consider what was very relevant to many employees prior to 2020. In the time leading up to the pandemic, two terms really come to mind when we think about accountability: *availability* and *visibility*.

We wanted to be seen when we were at work, and we all felt that to show our worth to our managers and teams, the tracked hours spent at work had a lot to do with our perceived accountability.

Regarding visibility, while research has indicated that a certain amount of presence is good for overall employee engagement and culture, prior to the pandemic, we all, including myself, felt a need to be very visible. Coffee runs, hallway conversations, team lunches, and, of course, the water-cooler chats, all played a role in culture. However, this also played a role in our perceived accountability. You're at the office. You're present. You've talked to several people. Your accountability is high, then, right? Not so much.

Prior to the pandemic, employee engagement was suffering. It had been on a steady decline, on average, and while some industries were still thriving, most professional services were not. What happened to all of us is that we switched out accountability with presenteeism. Mindtools (n.d.) defines presenteeism as "when you feel the need to work or do extra work just to be seen doing it, even if you are sick or otherwise not at your best." This phenomenon was (no pun intended) present and prevalent in pre-pandemic times. It is what was honored and expected.

Accountability didn't feel like the goal. Rather, we had placed unrealistic expectations of ourselves without taking care of ourselves too much, and those things really impacted our overall productivity and engagement, and our culture suffered.

As we started the pandemic, something remarkable happened. For many organizations, overall engagement improved, as did productivity. How could this be? For the first time in what feels like the history of humankind, people trusted that work would get done as bigger things around the world were happening. Everyone continued communicating (via technology), and work was getting done at a high rate. Sure, this could have been the nature of the world, where we said, "Well, there's nothing else to do but work and take care of my family during this time." But we were resilient, and we didn't need to be available or visible to show our accountability.

Brecheisen et al. (2002) at Gallup identified five items related to employee engagement that best differentiate the culture of resilient business units during disruptive times:

- Setting clear expectations

- Having the right materials and equipment

- Opportunities for employees to do what they do best

- Connection to the mission and purpose of the organization

- Coworkers who are committed to do quality work

As for our team at Gallup, where I work, we were able to set clear expectations of what was going to happen. We knew what our strategy needed to be in an environment where people might not be ready to necessarily spend, and we ensured we were ready to not only execute that plan, but also grow in our understanding of the data and insights that would help us optimize it throughout the course of the pandemic.

Our team was both forced and excited to develop their skills, and relied on their expertise to execute our strategy. The organization not only stuck to its values but doubled down on its values in providing unmatched analytics and advice to leaders. We were aligned and productive, and had great accountability thanks to our commitment to organizational culture. Some people liked to work from home and occasionally work in the office. Some people were just fine working full-time at home. Others felt the need to come in and couldn't stay away.

The aftermath of vaccination, and subsequently the severity of the pandemic, had so many questions that organizations, managers, and teams needed to consider and still need to face. The rest of this chapter is going to be dedicated to this.

Employee Engagement and Well-being within Hybrid and Remote Work

Here are a couple of statistics from a February 2022 study where Gallup researched over 12,000 employees in the US:

- 4 out of 10 US employees are hybrid or remote.

- 70% of these employees that would want to be hybrid would prefer to be fully remote.

The following are charts that look at remote-capable jobs, as well as engagement and burnout:

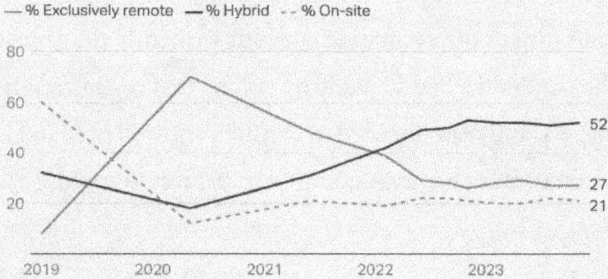

Work Locations for U.S. Employees With Remote-Capable Jobs

Employees are returning to the office — but with more remote work flexibility than ever.

— % Exclusively remote — % Hybrid - - % On-site

Data are among U.S. full-time, remote-capable employees.

GALLUP

Data is from "Hybrid work," by Gallup, n.d. (https://ww w.gallup.com/401384/indicator-hybrid-work.aspx). Copyright 2023 by Gallup.

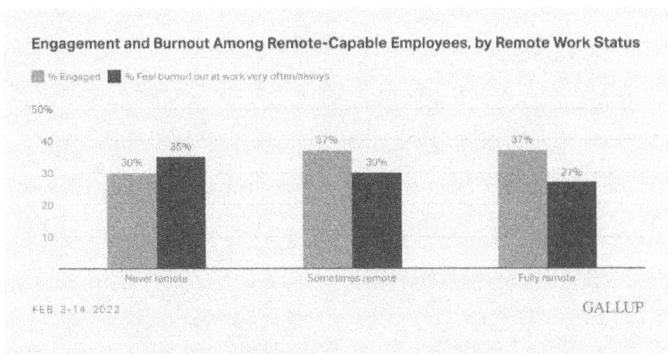

Engagement and Burnout Among Remote-Capable Employees, by Remote Work Status

% Engaged   % Feel burned out at work very often/always

	Never remote	Sometimes remote	Fully remote
% Engaged	30%	37%	37%
% Feel burned out	35%	30%	27%

FEB 3-14 2022   GALLUP

Data is from "The four essential dynamics of hybrid work" by J. Brecheisen, A. Truscott-Smith, and B. Wigert, 2022 (https://www.gallup.com/workplace/390944/four-essent ial-dynamics-hybrid-work.aspx). Copyright 2023 by Gallup.

Flexible work arrangements and 100% remote work can lead to a feeling of "never not working." People can feel they are "always on" because technology is there to provide you a way of answering email and responding to clients. There can be psychological and mental health issues that arise from being alone too long, always working, and not exhaling. How can organizations combat these issues, while striving for great accountability and productivity?

The answer I sought was within organizational culture. To get to the right culture, you might need to step back and address the evolution of the culture you had vs. the culture you are striving for.

To understand where we need to go, we can first consider potential benefits and challenges that come within a hybrid or remote work environment. The following graphics depict some statistics related to these benefits and challenges of hybrid work.

Advantages of Hybrid Work, Ranked by Most Common Response

Since you began your hybrid work arrangement, which of the following positive impacts on your work have you noticed? Select all that apply. (% Mentioning)

Top advantages

Improved work-life balance	71
More efficient use of time	67
Freedom to choose when and where I work	62
Less work burnout or fatigue	58
Higher productivity	51

Other advantages

Easier to coordinate work with teammates	22
Improved working relationship with coworkers	17
Increased team collaboration	16
Better cross-functional communication and collaboration	16
Better access to work resources and equipment	15
Better at meeting customer needs	13
More connected to organization's culture	11
Improved employee-manager relationship	11
More development opportunities	9
Easier to understand expectations and priorities	7
More feedback opportunities	6
More recognition	5

JUNE 13-23, 2022   GALLUP

Data is from "The advantages and challenges of hybrid work" by B. Wigert and J. White, 2022 (https://www.gallup.com/workplace/398135/advantages-challenges-hybrid-work.aspx). Copyright 2023 by Gallup.

Challenges of Hybrid Work, Ranked by Most Common Response

Since you began your hybrid work arrangement, which of the following negative impacts on your work have you noticed? Select all that apply. (% Mentioning)

Top challenges

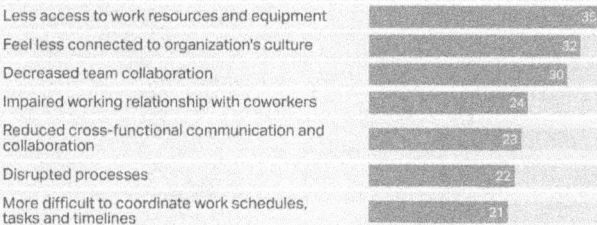

Challenge	%
Less access to work resources and equipment	35
Feel less connected to organization's culture	32
Decreased team collaboration	30
Impaired working relationship with coworkers	24
Reduced cross-functional communication and collaboration	23
Disrupted processes	22
More difficult to coordinate work schedules, tasks and timelines	21

Other challenges

Challenge	%
Fewer opportunities for feedback	19
Reduced work-life balance	16
Difficult to coordinate shared workspaces	15
Inefficient use of time	15
Decreased productivity	15
Less recognition	15
Impaired employee-manager relationship	13
More work burnout or fatigue	12
Fewer development opportunities	12
Unclear expectations and priorities	11
Less freedom to choose when and where I work	9
More challenging to meet customer needs	8

JUNE 13-23, 2022   GALLUP

Data is from "The advantages and challenges of hybrid work" by B. Wigert and J. White, 2022 (https://www.gallup.com/workplace/398135/advantages-challenges-hybrid-work.aspx). Copyright 2023 by Gallup.

What defined productivity and accountability in the past is what I believe needed to be changed to maintain effective employee engagement and well-being (the main one being hours worked). For years, we've always cared about the total amount of hours worked; that was, essentially, how long workers were at the office. We didn't have the ability to do a great job of recording hours worked (and we still might not), but the idea that hours at an office are the same thing as productive time felt antiquated, and the pandemic proved that. We were able to see people get their work done and have very effective conversations, and teams were able to thrive and strategize well.

Obviously, some roles are different from others, but for most white-collar roles, I have seen that people can thrive, thinking maybe they can do this "work-from-home thing" regularly. If people can do what they need to do, and not just show up, but thrive and go further, maybe there will be more to someone's drive than just hours worked.

Let's unpack this for a moment. If people aren't tied to hours, but somehow they are getting work done, having meaningful meetings and conversations, and growing in their own development, maybe tracking hours was holding them back?

I believe the one thing that organizations failed to realize, especially companies hiring college graduates and those with higher degrees, is that employees do want to seek more for themselves. That can't always be measured by hours worked, though, because the real value isn't total hours; it's outcomes and what is brought to the table.

The value is what is produced. This is what I think culturally changed about us, thanks to the pandemic. It doesn't matter how much time was spent. Value needs to be met based on the collective goals you have discussed with your manager and team.

A Great Manager Matters

As mentioned earlier, with fully hybrid or remote setups, employees felt the need to always be on. So, how can we avoid that? More importantly, how can we continually maintain and improve employee well-being, and help them sustain a great career in a hybrid or remote environment?

Understanding Your Strengths

As mentioned above, Brecheisen et al. (2002) identified five items related to employee engagement that best differentiate the culture of resilient business units during disruptive times:

- Setting clear expectations

- Having the right materials and equipment

- Opportunities for employees to do what they do best

- Connection to the mission and purpose of the organization

- Coworkers who are committed to do quality work

My firm belief is that a leader or manager is extremely important in ensuring the employee is getting what they need to lead a happy work life. This relates to a manager's relationship with their employee(s) and understanding of their strengths.

My own manager knows my strengths very well. Knowing my top strengths, as well as the experience she has in understanding me, she's created an environment based on my workstyle that benefits the group. She knows that I do well with autonomy. She understands that I do what is in the best interest of our team. She provides me with the tools and materials I need to achieve what needs to be done.

From what I've seen, effective leaders managing teams and employees in the hybrid and remote world will do this. They will continue to craft their strategy of leadership around what is best for their employees. There are great employees with many different strengths that benefit in more communication. Building the proper cadence with those individuals, as well as understanding the role of recognition, goes a long way to sustain a healthy hybrid or remote employee engagement.

Believe in Professionalism

I'm a firm believer that most professionals don't want to hand over a poor deliverable. They'll ask the questions needed, research the data that is required, and will do the extra things that will make them feel good about putting their name on their work. Managers have recognized this. They've seen that people could do quality work without constant supervision. They've recognized that employees value what they do.

Now, this isn't always the case. Some individuals will require much more oversight. So, how do you get those people to continue to work at a high level if they don't want to return to the office? How can we ensure remote employees are going to be engaged?

In Gallup's (n.d.) "Guide to Hybrid Working and Managing Remote Teams," there are four "basic drivers of employee engagement through the lens of remote work":

- Purpose: Where does my work fit within the company?

- Development: How is this going to continue to

grow my career in the company and overall?

- Caring management: Am I connecting with my manager and are they giving me great feedback and coaching, and caring about me as a person?

- Strengths focus: Are all the issues and roadblocks addressed so I can perform at my highest level?

I feel these result in improved culture, better collaboration, clearer understanding of available resources, increased coordination, and streamlined processes.

When a manager or leader thinks in terms of the above while believing in their employees, hybrid and remote work can really work long-term.

Grow Productivity and Accountability for Hybrid and Remote Employees

Since the beginning of this chapter, we've gone through what accountability has looked like, the role of employee engagement and well-being, and why a great manager matters. I'll now continue exploring the importance of great leadership, along with metrics, and how they can help sustain accountability.

The Manager

There is a need to set a regular cadence for meetings, and managers need to understand the strengths and nature of their employees and treat them as professionals. These are all important to build a good relationship with a hybrid or remote employee.

So, what is further needed? I believe in the importance of recognizing team goals that connect to the organization.

According to Hickman and Maese (2021), a manager is reported to be responsible for 70% of their team's engagement. In the United States, close to half of the population starts their day without a clear expectation of what to achieve. If managers and employees can set goals together to help employees reach those goals—and then showcase those outcomes—employees can feel much more confident about the approach they are taking in their work.

If accountability is the result of communication of expectations, review of performance, and reward and recognition of good performance, then there is no one better within organizations to achieve accountability than the manager. With this in mind, it is up to managers and other leaders within the organization to steward a culture that promotes accountability across the organization.

Great Metrics

In the world of hybrid and remote working, the number of hours worked is not a great way to show accountability. Instead, measuring goals reached is a far better way to think about employee productivity and accountability. The best organizations will connect business outcomes to the most important elements of a person's job.

This could be a slippery slope because it's not always the case that projects and goals will positively impact the bottom line. Yet, it is a good method to understand individual employee productivity. Specifically, you can do the following:

- Review goals of projects and other work completed, as well as milestones within goals

- Understand the role of those goals and projects to the bottom line of the company (e.g., revenue, or other key bottom-line KPIs)

The nice thing about goals and milestones is that there is a rationale based on the business results and the bottom line. Furthermore, there are things to celebrate, which can also inspire new ideas.

In 2020, I worked on a project and needed to show the value proposition of learning something, along with the application to our organization. My first step was to discuss with my manager why it was important to our team. I took the time to showcase the value proposition. This wasn't going to result in immediate return on investment (ROI). Milestones showed my progress. While I did track my hours, it didn't matter how fast or slow it took. What mattered was the goal of completion. Steady check-ins with my manager to review milestones measured progress.

The metrics here were mainly tied to the value proposition. At this point, we can tie in positive revenue and other metrics to these strategies, though these may not be immediate. Managers and employees, therefore, need to consider what are the most appropriate metrics.

Conclusion

To sustain accountability and productivity in a hybrid or remote world, it takes ownership between the organization, managers, and employees. Organizations need to be flexible.

Managers need to foster the values and goals of the organization. Managers need to understand the strengths of employees, treat them as professionals, and keep up with them individually.

Through this relationship, managers and employees will come together to understand projects, goals, and milestones, which can be discussed at regular intervals, and that can be traced to the organization's bottom line. This helps ensure a connection between the employees' work and the bigger picture. In turn, this helps foster culture and connection to the organization.

References

Brecheisen, J., Truscott-Smith, A., & Wigert, B. (2022, March 31). *The Four essential dynamics of hybrid work.* Gallup. https://www.gallup.com/workplace/390944/four-essential-dynamics-hybrid-work.aspx

Gallup. (n.d.). *Hybrid work.* https://www.gallup.com/401384/indicator-hybrid-work.aspx

Gallup. (n.d.). *A guide to hybrid work and managing a remote team.* https://www.gallup.com/workplace/316313/understanding-and-managing-remote-workers.aspx

Hickman, A., & Maese, E. (2021, March 26). Measure performance: Strategies for remote and hybrid teams. Gallup. https://www.gallup.com/workplace/341894/measure-performance-strategies-remote-hybrid-teams.aspx

MindTools. (n.d.). *Showing up for the sake of it.* https://ww
w.mindtools.com/a1emfwe/presenteeism

Wigert, B., & White, J. (2022, September 14).
The advantages and challenges of hybrid work.
Gallup. https://www.gallup.com/workplace/398135/adva
ntages-challenges-hybrid-work.aspx

Chapter Seven

How to be Fair in a World with Proximity Bias

Nadia Harris

Introduction and Definition of Proximity Bias

Hybrid work is on the rise. It's supposed to be a win-win solution. Companies all around the world have rushed into announcing their hybrid working policies aiming for more workplace flexibility. Having worked with numerous hybrid companies from around the world, I can clearly state that such an approach would not succeed if it were implemented without a strategy and change management. Why? Because there will be several challenges, including proximity bias. Proximity bias is the tendency to favor individuals who are physically or socially closer, leading to exclusion of individuals who are not in close proximity.

Increasing working hours became mainstream within the corporate world. Office attendance was confused with productivity and engagement. Arriving early and leaving late was favored by managers and supervisors. At the end of the day, proximity bias actually becomes the culprit of employee disengagement, dissatisfaction, and burnout, especially in a hybrid team. In hybrid teams, physical proximity may happen if some team members attend the office more often than others, or if a company is shaped so there are both office and remote workers as part of the team. In this case, proximity bias may become the main factor in determining who is included or excluded.

What's more, proximity bias can also manifest in other ways, such as favoring individuals who work in the same time zone or who use the same communication tools. Interestingly, I have observed several concerning hybrid working expectations that required team members to always remain seated in front of their laptops so that company-wide tracking software could confirm their virtual presence. There are also other examples too, such as judging whether someone is working or not based on their status color in communication apps.

It's not hard to imagine a situation where managers believe that office-based employees work harder than remote ones. Supervisors assume that since they can see staff working, the "invisible" remote ones are not as engaged or efficient as the ones in the office. It's an unconscious tendency to favor people who are physically closer or even "virtually closer," if managers constantly check whether remote workers are online and moving their mouse on the screen. Physical proximity can make it much easier for employees to be recognized by their managers in terms of salary increases, promotion, or career development.

Understanding the Origin of Proximity Bias

Proximity bias can be traced back to human evolution and the need for survival. In prehistoric times, humans lived in small, close-knit communities where cooperation and collaboration were necessary for survival. In these communities, people tended to trust and favor those who were physically close to them, as these were the individuals they relied on for protection, food, and other crucial resources. This instinctual bias toward people who are physically close has become known as proximity bias, and it has persisted throughout human history. What's more, it's still prevalent in modern society.

In addition to evolution, social psychology also plays a role in proximity bias. The social identity theory shows that people derive part of their sense of identity and self-worth from the groups they belong to. When people are physically close to others who share similar characteristics or experiences, they are more likely to feel a sense of belonging and validation. Consequently, this can reinforce proximity bias and lead to exclusion or discrimination. It can also have significant negative impacts on productivity, innovation, and diversity. As such, it's important for organizations to recognize and address proximity bias in order to promote a more inclusive and equitable workplace.

Cognitive Bias

One form of proximity bias is cognitive bias. This is a concept in psychology and decision-making that refers to the systematic errors in thinking that can occur when people process information. There's a tendency to think in a way that is not entirely rational or objective and can lead to inaccurate judgments, beliefs, and behaviors, and it can manifest itself in numerous ways. Hence, we can distinguish many types of cognitive biases, including confirmation bias, where people seek out information that confirms their existing beliefs, and availability bias, where people rely on the most easily available information to make decisions. Other types of cognitive biases include anchoring bias, where people rely too heavily on the first piece of information they receive, and the bandwagon effect, where people adopt certain beliefs or behaviors simply because others around them are doing the same.

Proximity bias is also a form a cognitive bias because it's based on limited information and can lead to unfair treatment of individuals who are not physically close. People may assume that those who are close to them are more competent, trustworthy, or likable, even if they have no evidence to support these assumptions. Consequently, they may assume that those who are not physically close are less competent or less invested in the work, leading to exclusion or discrimination.

Cognitive Biases and Decision-Making

Cognitive biases can affect decision-making in a variety of settings, including personal relationships, politics, and business. They can also have significant implications for how organizations operate, particularly in areas such as hiring, promotion, performance evaluation, or even project planning. We can come across managers who have a positive impression of an employee and may rate them higher on all aspects of their performance evaluation, even if some areas are actually weaker than others. At the same time, the risk of cognitive biases negatively impacting distributed teams gets even bigger. Let me share a few examples.

Team members who work together in an office may form a closer bond and develop stronger relationships, leading to an "in-group" bias where they prioritize the needs and opinions of their office-based colleagues over those who work remotely. This leads to excluding remote team members and creating a disconnect within a team. Such a situation will then directly impact aspects such as company culture.

Another example can be when office workers have more access to company-wide information, project progress and updates. We may then observe "anchoring" bias, as opinions and decisions of physically present employees will be given more importance and weight during the collaboration process. Remote workers may not get a chance to equally contribute to teamwork, as cognitive biases will start ruling the overall cooperation experience.

One of the challenges of cognitive biases is that they often occur unconsciously, meaning that people are not aware that their thinking is biased. However, it's possible to reduce the impact of cognitive biases through techniques such as mindfulness, cognitive restructuring, and diverse perspectives. By recognizing the ways in which our thinking can be biased and taking steps to address these biases, we can make better decisions and create a more equitable and just workplace.

In other words, cognitive biases are around us in our everyday lives. They are mental shortcuts that our brains use to make decisions quickly, often based on incomplete or inaccurate information. While, in some situations, cognitive biases may be helpful, in a hybrid workplace they can lead to errors in judgment or discriminatory behavior among workers.

Proximity Bias and Hybrid Work Failure

As I have just explained above, proximity bias can have significant impacts on decision-making, interpersonal relationships, and organizational culture. It's worth looking at this topic from an even broader perspective, as hybrid work should be evaluated in terms of scalability and other important workplace metrics, such as diversity. Employees who work remotely, or in different locations, may come from different backgrounds, have different perspectives, and bring different skills and experiences to the table. Proximity bias can lead to a lack of diversity in the workplace, which can limit creativity, innovation, problem-solving abilities, and opportunities for individuals who are not in close physical or social proximity to those in positions of power. This can perpetuate systems of inequality and discrimination, leading to a less diverse and less inclusive workplace or community.

In terms of company culture, proximity bias can perpetuate a culture of exclusion or favoritism. A good example can be a workplace where managers favor employees who work in the same office or department. These employees may have greater access to resources, opportunities for advancement, and social connections, leading to a culture of unequal opportunities and exclusivity. Addressing proximity bias in a hybrid company culture requires a proactive and intentional effort to create a culture of inclusion and to leverage technology to promote collaboration and communication. Companies should establish clear communication protocols and ensure that feedback and performance evaluations are based on objective criteria rather than physical presence.

The Importance of Trust

Another essential element that can make or break a distributed team is trust. When team members are working remotely, trust becomes very important because they cannot rely on face-to-face interactions to build relationships and establish trust. Effective communication cannot happen without it. When team members trust each other, they are more likely to share information openly and honestly, which leads to better collaboration and decision-making. Additionally, trust is the foundation of strong relationships at work. If trust is present, it's much easier to achieve common goals. Employees feel more satisfied with their work and their team as they are able to collaborate efficiently and effectively. Team members can rely on each other to complete tasks and meet deadlines, which leads to increased productivity and better results.

Now, let's imagine that we are dealing with a hybrid team without trust. Managers rely only on what they see, and do not take into account the fact that they tend to favor team members being in physical proximity. What is going to happen, most probably, is a toxic situation, where on-site managers may feel the need to micromanage the work of remote workers, constantly checking in and monitoring their progress. This can create a sense of distrust and resentment among remote team members, and lead to decreased productivity and overall job satisfaction.

In the 2022 Edelman Trust Barometer Special Report, "Trust in the Workplace," we find that trust is directly linked to increased loyalty, employee advocacy, commitment, and engagement. This data makes it very tempting for me to claim that it's not fancy office perks, free Friday lunches, or billiard tables that build a great working culture. It's something much more meaningful that connects individuals with the company.

Mitigating Proximity Bias in Hybrid Teams

Mitigating proximity bias in hybrid teams requires intentional effort and a combination of various strategies. We cannot possibly try to fix something if we do not understand what is broken. That is the reason we should first and foremost raise awareness of the issue, and this can only happen if we start educating the whole organization about it. Everyone must be on board to make this happen. In other words, spreading awareness about proximity bias is the first step to making sure it gets eliminated in favor of equal treatment among office-based and remote team members.

Understanding how proximity bias manifests itself in the hybrid workplace and its negative impact on productivity, collaboration, and diversity is the first step to successfully overcoming it. To do it, the company can introduce training sessions or different resources to share information about how this issue impacts team dynamics. It's also a good idea to start sharing various techniques that will help the team reflect on their own behaviors and perceptions they have in the workplace. The goal is to introduce a multifaceted approach that addresses the underlying causes of such bias. By establishing objective criteria, using blind screening techniques, offering remote work opportunities, encouraging virtual communication, and promoting diversity and inclusion, companies can reduce the impact of proximity bias and create a more equitable and inclusive workplace.

Companies that have successfully implemented strategies to overcome proximity bias have several things in common. These can be, for example, encouraging video calls instead of emails, setting up virtual water coolers for employees to connect with each other, or having team members visit each other in person from time to time. This eliminates distance and ensures a highly collaborative and inclusive work culture.

Successful Practices to Address Proximity Bias

In terms of great practices, it's worth considering the practices of a remote-first company that has successfully addressed proximity bias, Buffer. Buffer ensures that all employees feel included thanks to tools like Donut in Slack that randomly pairs employees for virtual coffee chats. The company also encourages their team members to share personal stories and engage in social activities like a virtual game night or book clubs. The goal is to foster a sense of community and belonging among all employees that consequently creates a more inclusive working environment.

In terms of hybrid companies, it's worth looking at Microsoft, which has successfully implemented several strategies that include training programs aimed at teaching employees how to recognize and overcome their unconscious biases. The company openly encourages remote work and flexible schedules by making it a policy that allows employees to work from wherever they feel most comfortable. They have explicit communication and clear rules that help the entire company emphasize working results rather than physical presence. Such transparency is crucial to build a scalable, bias-free hybrid working approach that ensures equal treatment for all employees. If companies simply agree for people to work from home without any clear principles or expectations, outdated working patterns, such as physical presence prevailing over remote work, will likely succeed.

If I had to summarize several straightforward techniques that can help overcome proximity bias in a hybrid team, I would stress team discipline and encourage proactivity and social events. Sometimes even the smallest steps can work wonders, and it's just a matter of goodwill to successfully tackle a big problem.

The Importance of Social Events

Now, let me elaborate some on social events. It's a popular misconception that remote workers never meet in real life and just use online messaging to collaborate. However, this is not true, as well-known distributed companies stress the necessity of in-person meetings. Social events play an important role in creating a sense of community and strengthening relationships within hybrid teams. Social events provide an opportunity for team members to get to know each other on a more personal level, and this inevitably leads to strengthened relationships. In a hybrid team, people do not have the opportunity to interact with each other in person on a regular basis. Such events can lead to fostering teamwork because they build a sense of camaraderie and team spirit, which can improve collaboration. The goal is for team members to feel connected and invested in each other's success. If this happens, we can be assured that, if they start collaborating in a distributed environment, they will work closely together toward achieving mutual goals.

A team's morale is also an especially important aspect, and social events can have a great impact, as team members have fun and unwind together. This will also trigger a sense of belonging and getting closer to one another so that, even if they do not see each other daily, the team will remember those

143

great moments of being together and they will feel a deeper connection that they truly are a team.

It's no secret that technology is essential to communicating in a hybrid setup thanks to tools such as video conferencing, instant messaging, and collaboration software. Such tools enable teams to communicate in real time to share information and collaborate on different projects. What is important is full transparency to make sure that all team members are equally equipped for success in terms of their daily performance. I would strongly advise using tools like Google Drive or Microsoft Teams so employees can work on documents and files together in real time. All processes and expectations will be stored in a mutually accessible place for all workers, whether they are on-site or remote.

Using Technology to Track Productivity and Progress

In terms of productivity and tracking progress, technology can help teams by automating routine tasks and streamlining workflows. Managers can then have a full overview of what is happening, what the blockers are, and how each team member is performing daily. There are different project management applications available, such as Trello, Monday, and Jira, so teams can stay organized and on track with their work.

Such tracking tools can help workers stay accountable and manage their tasks effectively. Most importantly, what can be achieved here is clear visibility on what is happening in terms of daily work activities, so managers do not have to ask questions and make assumptions about false performance and engagement. Of course, we cannot and shouldn't forget about the important aspect of data analysis and how technology can help hybrid teams in this aspect. Tools such as business intelligence software and data visualization tools can help teams analyze data to identify trends, make predictions, and optimize performance.

In summary, technology is essential for hybrid teams to communicate, collaborate, stay productive, be flexible, and analyze data. By leveraging technology effectively, hybrid teams can work together seamlessly and achieve their goals.

Objectivity in the Workplace

Objectivity in the workplace is essential for fair and equitable treatment of all employees. We can describe it as the ability to make unbiased, impartial, and rational decisions based on facts, evidence, and merit, rather than personal preferences, prejudices, or other irrelevant factors. In an objective workplace, all employees are evaluated and treated fairly, regardless of their gender, race, ethnicity, age, religion, or any other personal characteristic.

Lack of objectivity in the workplace can lead to unfair treatment of employees, discrimination, and biased decision-making. This can literally affect every area of the business. Let us imagine biased hiring and promotion processes. The results could be dramatic if managers relied on personal connections or subjective judgments rather than objective criteria to make such decisions. We may run into situations where these managers are biased against qualified candidates who don't fit their personal preferences or biases. For example, a manager might favor a worker who has had the same hobby that they have discussed several times during in-person meetings. The same worker may be much less qualified for the job than a remote worker who has never had the opportunity to spend quality, in-person time with the manager.

Conclusion

Spreading awareness about proximity bias and the necessity to remain objective in the workplace refers not only to the leadership team, but also to all managers as well as all workers who interact with each other on a daily basis. One of the most important roles here is the engagement of the HR department so that designing bias-free processes, transparent feedback frameworks, and performance evaluations becomes part of a broader change management process to also generate a mindset shift across the company.

All in all, proximity bias can trigger severe problems in hybrid teams. Therefore, it's essential to speak about it openly and establish a data-oriented approach to ensure objectivity. Hybrid companies cannot forget about virtual colleagues who need a fair chance to succeed and remain connected.

Section V – Human Capital

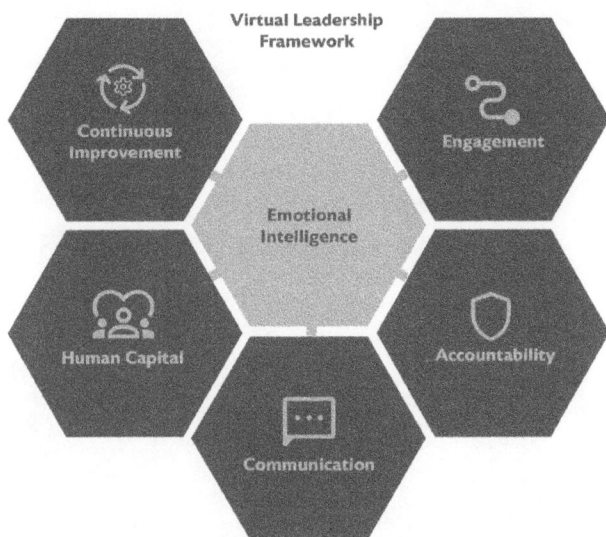

WINNING IN THE VIRTUAL WORKPLACE

Chapter Eight

The Personal Side of Project Management in the Virtual Workplace

William J. Quinn, III

"**B**eing a Project Manager is like being an artist, you have the different colored process streams combining into a work of art" (Cimmarrusti, 2018). Being a project manager in a virtual setting is like being an artist where colors can come from all over the world, at all times of the day, and land on a canvas that you have never even seen.

Project management has existed throughout time. While the exact methodology may be a bit of a mystery, it is clear that things such as the Pyramids of Egypt, the Great Wall of China, and the road systems of the Romans took acquiring, managing, and coordinating a vast number of resources. While these are giant examples (literally), project management doesn't always involve massive undertakings. The Project Management Institute (PMI) stated that a project is "a temporary group activity designed to produce a unique product, service or result" (Project Management Institute, 2013). Successfully achieving this result requires the use and coordination of resources with definitive start and end points.

We've all acted as informal project members throughout our lives. Planning a wedding, purchasing a home, designing landscaping, and decorating our living spaces all require some level of project management. There is some debate as to exactly when formal project management came into existence, but it can be traced at least back to the early 1950s when it was specifically mentioned in the Atlas missile project (Morris & Hough,1987). Project management is currently one of the fastest growing careers domestically and internationally. Not only is it a naturally growing field, but we are also experiencing the first generation of project managers—those baby-boomer pioneers of the industry who started in the

1950s and 1960s—reaching retirement age and exiting the market.

While, historically, project management has been most prevalent in industries such as construction, information technology (IT), and engineering, we are seeing a rise in less traditional settings including healthcare, manufacturing, and even the legal world. This diversity of industry is helping to drive the growth. While the Bureau of Labor Statistics is projecting a minimum growth rate of over 7% per year in the United States for the next decade, this demand is not limited to the United States. Project managers may be in even higher demand internationally. The PMI reported the demand for project management professionals in other countries, including China, India, Japan, Germany, and the United Kingdom is also growing. They predict there will be 60 million openings internationally over the next five years.

Virtual Project Management

The combination of the rise in demand for project management, both domestically and internationally, and the continued rise of the virtual workforce results in a very favorable outlook for the future of remote project management. There are several aspects that can aid you in your quest to be a successful project manager in a remote setting. Communication, time management, organizational awareness, and leadership skills, all of which I will touch on later, are very important in the project management world. However, I would argue that the most critical factor for success is your choice of organization. Despite the rise of the virtual workplace, many companies are still attempting, with varying success, to get employees back in the office. So, if the remote aspect of virtual project management is important to you, be sure to ask in-depth questions about not only the current remote work environment, but also the planned future of their virtual presence.

Once you have established the organization is committed to a virtual setting, the next thing to consider is by what factors your success will be determined. The results-oriented work environment (ROWE) was first introduced by Best Buy in 2005, but since then many companies, both large and small, have adopted this system (Peek, 2023). In this type of workplace, effectiveness is based on results, performance, and output, rather than the number of hours spent completing a task. This is important because when managing projects virtually, your team may not necessarily be on the same schedule or even in the same time zone. You must be able to assign and monitor tasks occurring simultaneously on multiple different timetables. If you work for a company that is more worried about your scheduled availability (i.e., a "9–5 job"), you would either need to put in extra hours to compensate for the virtual environment or waste a lot of time by attempting to communicate and coordinate tasks asynchronously. Working for an organization that understands and appreciates that results count makes project management a much easier and more rewarding task.

The Importance of Team Building

Once you find yourself working for an organization that you are comfortable with, the next step is team building. If you are lucky enough to select your team, do so wisely. Choose people who have a strong knowledge base with respect to their anticipated tasks, thrive with your communication style, and, above all, are trustworthy. Other than your employer, your team will be the most important factor determining your success or failure as a project manager.

We are not always fortunate enough to pick our teams, though. Frequently we are assigned staff members with whom we must work. When this happens, we have to rely on our core competencies in the basics of project management: communication, time management, organizational aware-ness, problem-solving, and leadership skills. These skills are considered the five pillars of project management, each of which requires a different application in the virtual setting than they do in a traditional work environment. Each will now be explored.

Communication

Communication is listed first because it is absolutely critical and affects your ability to function within the other four pillars (time management, organizational awareness, problem-solving, and leadership skills). When it comes to communication in the traditional workplace, there are a few staples in which almost all of us have participated. When we are in the office we email, call by phone, or instant message in some form, but face-to-face interactions are among the biggest forms of communication. In a physical workspace, such face-time experiences can help to build rapport with your team members. These may be through formal means, such as group meetings or scheduled one-on-ones, and allow for a rapid exchange of information in a controlled manner and can give you an idea of how your coworkers give and receive information.

There are also ample opportunities for informal face-to-face interactions, such as water-cooler talk, where you get to know your coworkers and team members on a more personal level. Whether it is what they did over the weekend, what books they are reading, what shows they are watching, or just what they do for fun, all of this gives insight into who they are as a person, and it gives them insight into who you are.

These factors help to create a non-working bond which can increase the effectiveness of communication. The challenge in the virtual workplace is fostering these same bonds without the benefit of just bumping into each other throughout the day. How do we mimic these interactions in a virtual setting? The answer is that there is no one answer.

Here are some tips for effective communication in the virtual workspace:

- Have "getting to know you" meetings

- Encourage spontaneous conversations

- Document

Have "Getting to Know You" Meetings

Effective communication in a virtual setting takes effort, planning, and coordination. As a project manager in a virtual setting, your effort is critical in fostering good communication. Despite the fact that there will be a lot of asynchronous information exchange directly related to the project at hand, there should also be a good amount of synchronous conversations with the goal of building trust and reinforcing relationships. Fortunately, we have a plethora of tools available to us that can help with this connection. Whether it be video meetings, texts, phone calls, or instant messages, you need to find ways to learn about your team and give them ample opportunities to learn about you. This is where regularly scheduled (and respectfully scheduled) meetings can be a big help. One-on-one video conversations are a great way to develop relationships with your team, especially near the beginning of a project. These give you the opportunity to learn more about the individuals with whom you are working. Schedule these as informational exchange sessions, but also make sure that you take the time to connect on a personal level.

I try to break these meetings into three distinct phases. For the first phase, act as if you are at the water cooler and just bumped into your colleague. Ask open-ended, leading questions. Ask about their day, their family, their weekend, anything other than just the work that you share. Likewise, take the time to discuss some of your personal factors, letting them get to know you, as well. This type of two-way communication can go far toward building trust. For the second part of the meeting, I focus on discussing the project from their perspective. This gives you the ability to find out how they are doing on their tasks, and how they feel about the project and the team in general. The final phase is reserved for giving direction and explaining any changes to the plan.

Encourage Spontaneous Conversations

In addition to these scheduled sessions, I suggest being as available as possible for spontaneous conversations. It helps to be online, or available on a regular schedule (if possible), and to let your team know these scheduled times of availability. These can be accomplished via direct message, text, video chats, or good old-fashioned phone calls. The method isn't important, but the message is, and that message is you are interested in your team and ready to connect with them.

In conjunction with getting-to-know-your-team-type communication, you will also need informational-exchange-type communication. Regularly scheduled, formal meetings are a great way to keep the team informed and up to date. This can be a challenge with different time zones, but as a virtual project manager, it will be in your best interest to make meetings like this work within the confines of everyone's schedule.

Document

Keeping clear records of interactions should also be a big part of all project management meetings. Even the best coordinator in the world will not be able to assure 100% attendance to every meeting. Vacations, conflicting meetings, and emergencies (both work and personal) will result in people missing the occasional meeting. To combat this, detailed meeting minutes should be kept and made readily available to all team members. This allows absentees to catch up at their convenience and saves time by reducing the need to re-discuss items that have already been addressed.

Meeting minutes are not the only information that should be readily available in order to assure good communication. As a project manager you should maintain a library of all documents related to the project in a well-organized, easily accessible manner. I suggest using a shared drive in the cloud (such as Dropbox). Giving team members this type of access can reduce downtime while they wait for information that they may have had to otherwise request from a team member working on a different time schedule.

Time Management

Scheduling these formal and informal meetings, as well as having regular availability, require a high level of time-management skills. When working in an office setting, frequently your team members are all in the same building at the same time. When working in the virtual world, your team can be physically spread out and have drastically different work schedules. This poses challenges that a strong project manager must deal with and overcome to succeed. A critical factor to remember here is that you are not necessarily managing time, but rather managing people. To that end, you need to make sure that you and your team are set up for success.

Here are some tips for effective time management in the virtual workspace:

- Have a designated workspace

- Schedule time to communicate

- Track time

Have a Designated Workspace

First and foremost, a designated workspace is a great help for managing time. If you and your team treat your respective workspaces like you would a physical off-site office, it makes it easier to not be distracted, thereby making better use of your time. While many may not want to hear this, I also strongly suggest getting dressed for work, even if you aren't leaving the house. It makes it easier to get into a work mindset and mentality.

Schedule Time to Communicate

This applies to both group meetings and one-on-ones. Schedule task completion times, then be sure to track the time spent in each of these, and put the effort into completing each item in the allotted timeframe. We have all been in meetings that have gotten out of control and gone overtime; I doubt that many of us enjoyed them. Keep your meetings and sessions on topic. If you find them wandering or getting out of control, take charge and reset the path. If critical unanticipated issues come up during the meeting, still do what you can to end the session on time and simply add in another meeting at a later date. This gives everyone time to manage their own schedule and workload while still addressing issues as they arise.

Related to this is assigning duties and tasks. When doing so, be sure to consider the time already allotted for communication and meetings, existing workloads, and critical timelines; disrespecting the boundaries of your team is a good way to lose their trust. Tools such as shared calendars, project management software, and MS Teams are great ways to coordinate these schedules.

Track Time

If you do not monitor how your time is spent, it can be very easily wasted. This can be a daunting task for a project manager because you have to do it for yourself, as well as (at least to some extent) for your team members. With a small team, you may be able to keep track of time and activities via the use of a simple spreadsheet. However, if you have a larger team, or multiple teams, I strongly suggest moving to a project-management-based software package. Regardless of your choice, always remember to give your team access to the data.

Organizational Awareness

To interact with, coordinate, and get the most out of your team, you must be in tune with them. Organizational awareness is a widely used term, with many accepted meanings, so it can be somewhat of an esoteric topic. With respect to project management, it can be further focused to team awareness. This particular skill can be expressed as an understanding of the formal and informal interactions of the team and how these interactions can affect performance. In short, having a good understanding of your people and their motivations, strengths, weaknesses, communication styles, and work habits, as well as many other factors, can have a significant impact on the success (or failure) of the team.

Here are some tips for effective organizational awareness in the virtual workspace:

- Take the time to know your team.

- Use two-way communication.

- Understand the fit.

Take the Time to Know Your Team

We do not always have the luxury of choosing our own team. Frequently, we are assigned people and have the responsibility of molding them into a cohesive unit. The first step in the building process is to communicate with your team and help them grow. A great area to focus this growth on is in developing the decision-making process of your team. A good project manager will not only gather the data and make decisions but will also take the time to get everyone's opinion and garner buy-in from the team before choosing a path to be followed. Doing these things in a virtual setting can be difficult.

Use Two-Way Communication

Gathering opinions and information, as well as assessing the level of buy-in can be difficult when you aren't face-to-face. As a result, you may miss nonverbal clues that people can unconsciously give off when they are not in agreement. While it may sound simplistic, the only counter for this is a high level of two-way communication. There are two aspects to communication—the sending and receiving of the intended message. As a project manager in a virtual setting, you must take the extra time to assure that your team understands your message and that you understand theirs.

Understand the Fit

When I speak of understanding the fit, I am referring to how your team fits into the organization as a whole, and making sure that the team does, as well. While one of the major aspects of being a servant leader is putting your team members above the organization, you need to remember that the goal of the team is still to provide a service to the organization. For that to happen effectively and efficiently, you will be exchanging information with people outside of your team. You must keep this in mind and remind your team that, despite the fact that they may not see the higher-ups in the organization on a daily basis, they are still there and still expect results.

Problem-Solving

Even after you have chosen your organization, developed your team, become the leader you would want to follow, communicated effectively, and planned your project in a well-documented, readily accessible manner, there is still an important factor to remember. That is, problems will surely arise. It is always safe to assume that your plan is not perfect and that no project goes off without a few unanticipated issues arising.

How you deal with, and ultimately solve, these problems can make or break you as a project manager.

Here are some tips for effective problem-solving in the virtual workspace:

- Include your team

- Reach out for resources

- Document

Include Your Team

One of the best ways to deal with issues when they arise is to include your team almost from the very beginning. Brainstorming can be a fantastic tool. While as a leader you may have a tendency to fix things and move on, getting everyone's perspective can not only result in solutions that you may not have thought of yourself, but also help with garnering the buy-in that was discussed earlier in the chapter. However, I do not suggest that you jump right into a brainstorming meeting as soon as a problem arises. It is better to make the team aware of the problem and give them all time to think about and research solutions on their own time before bringing the team together. This not only shows that you have respect for their time, but also helps to make the brainstorming session as effective as possible.

Reach Out for Resources

While your team is researching their ideas, you should be doing the same. Bringing up problems without also offering solutions is very close to complaining, and nobody likes a complainer! This is where you as the team leader should reach out to the larger organization as a whole to see what resources are available that may benefit your team and, possibly more importantly, if these similar problems have been addressed in your organization in the past.

Applying these steps doesn't differ drastically between a traditional and a virtual setting, but the methods of communicating during the process can be very different. In a virtual setting, we cannot simply walk over to a coworker's office to see if their team faced similar challenges and, if so, how they dealt with them. What we can do is treat our coworkers as a part of a larger team and apply the same principles of communication to them as we do our own team. To be precise, research the issue on your own first so that you have some ideas to share. Then utilize whatever communication tools your organization makes available to you and schedule a meeting at a convenient time with coworkers who may be able to help. Once you have done this, you can bring your findings back to your team and integrate this information with the potential solutions that they may have come up with.

Document

A final step that should not be neglected is to document whatever solution your team decides upon and make the notes on it readily available. As discussed earlier, in the virtual setting, your team may need access to data at times when it isn't necessarily easy or appropriate to reach out to other team members. Having clear, readily accessible documentation allows them to get the knowledge they need to continue to work effectively. Additionally, if you have documentation readily available for others within your organization, they may be able to overcome obstacles without ever having to involve you or your team.

Leadership

As we've explored so far, project management requires competency in communication, time management, organizational awareness, and problem-solving. In addition, you must be a good leader to your team. The method of leadership that I have found to be most successful as a project leader is servant leadership. As a project manager (or any manager), you are trying to get your team to accomplish goals in the best way they see fit, without micromanaging them. A basic tenant of servant leadership is to encourage people to think for themselves while giving them the tools to follow through on their thought process (Nauman et al., 2022).

Here are some tips for effective leadership in the virtual workspace:

- Focus on people.

- Assure effective communication.

- Address behaviors.

- Provide stewardship.

Focus on People

Servant leadership requires you to focus on your team and put them first, as opposed to the needs of the company. A major aspect of leadership is how one keeps the team on track and completes tasks. The servant leader must rely on inspiring their followers as opposed to the more authoritative tools common in a command-and-control style of leadership. In one of the most widely accepted papers on servant leadership, Spears (2010) listed ten characteristics required for someone to lead in this manner; these characteristics are

listening, awareness, empathy, healing, persuasion, stewardship, building community, being dedicated to the growth of
people, conceptualization, and foresight.

Listening, empathy, and awareness are listed first, and with
good reason. Truly listening to what your team members
say, whether verbally, nonverbally, or just in their overall demeanor, can help the project manager address minor issues
before they escalate into major detriments. Being aware of, or
working to discover, the underlying reasons that team members are saying what they are saying can give you true insight as
to someone's mental or emotional state. Trying to empathize
with why team members feel the way that they do can help
you identify what you need to do as a servant to help them
get back to a highly functioning level.

Needless to say, truly listening, practicing awareness, and being empathetic can be difficult in any setting, but even more
so in the remote world. Visual and informal interactions in
a virtual setting are often constrained. Due to the brief du-
ration and formal structure, individuals may find it easier to
conceal their fatigue or frustration, given the restricted time
and methods for interacting with others.

Assure Effective Communication

A good virtual manager must make the effort to assure that effective communication is occurring. There should be frequent one-on-ones during which you ask probing questions while actively listening to what is said, what is not said, and, possibly most importantly, how it is being said. As a virtual project manager, in addition to discussing jobs and tasks, I try to have conversations designed to assess my team members' perceived level of motivation, and any sense of cynicism they may have. This leads to the healing and persuasion aspects of servant leadership.

Address Behaviors

Listening, empathy, and awareness will help you identify issues, but how you deal with them can be even more important. When I sense that negative performance factors seem to be increasing, I take the time to have a conversation about it, and then I am cognizant of the need for downtime for the team member. I encourage them to do something that refreshes them, so that they can have more positive energy with the project. I have also found that when these negative characteristics start to appear, that is frequently due to an imbalance in their work and personal life. To combat this, I find it helps to take the time to review, reinforce, and possibly reset boundaries.

If you find that a team member is putting in extraordinary hours, or even a disproportionately high level of effort to the point that it is becoming detrimental to their performance and well-being, then it may be time to intervene and help with the healing process. This could be as simple as making downtime a requirement of their job. An easy example is getting them to put a limit on hours that they can send or respond to asynchronous messages. I have found that when team members are reading and responding to emails or messages during their off hours, that they have frequently put too much focus on the work portion of their life to the detriment of other things that make them happy. By limiting the hours they put into work, you give them more time to do the things they enjoy; they may be more focused during their work hours, as well.

Some people do not react well to these kinds of limitations; that is when the persuasion skills come into play. As stated earlier, command-and-control tools aren't easily incorporated into servant leadership. So rather than tell them they cannot respond to emails during certain times, you must convince them that it is best for them and their loved ones and the project as a whole. This may not be an easy task, especially for high performers. I suggest being direct, communicating to the team member specific examples of how their performance has suffered, and focusing on the benefits of rest and downtime. Hopefully, you have developed a good connection with this person and, as a result, you can suggest they focus on some of their favorite hobbies or spending time with friends and family. This focus on your team members also ties into stewardship, building community, and being dedicated to the growth of people. These concepts are very closely tied together, so much so that it may be difficult to decide where one ends and the next begins.

Provide Stewardship

At the most fundamental level, stewardship is taking care of something or someone. In the case of servant leadership, it is caring for the needs of your team members above, but not in lieu of, the organization as a whole. Taking care of or caring for your team's needs very easily ties into being dedicated to their growth. If you have a team that you genuinely care about, you should genuinely want them to be the best they can be. This means dedicating resources, most importantly your time and energy, to giving them what they need to succeed at this level, as well as elevating their performance.

I have always believed that good leaders build teams, while great leaders build more leaders. When you are a successful steward of your team, and you are dedicated to their growth, it helps to build their trust in you. If this level of trust is strong and prevalent with all of your team members, it gives them a common motivation and a common ideal around which they can bond, thus building community. A community of leaders who care about each other is a team that is well-positioned for success.

How do we focus on these factors in a virtual setting as opposed to a more traditional one? Again, the answer is putting effort into communication and connection. This can be done through any of the means already mentioned above, as well as any others that you can think of.

Finally, a word about conceptualization and foresight. Conceptualization and foresight are factors that move focus away from people specifically, and more toward operational goals. Conceptualization can be regarded as the ability to look at the big picture without getting bogged down with details. By doing this, it allows you to develop strategies that should be effective in meeting team goals. Foresight will allow you to make judgment calls as to the likely success or failure of these strategies.

Conclusion

The message I have tried to convey is that project management is more about your team members than the project itself. To succeed as a project manager, you need to put at least as much time and energy into connecting with your people as you do on the project itself. You must make the effort to communicate, build connections, and then communicate even more to strengthen those connections. This cycle will help you build trust, build your team members' skill sets, and, ultimately, build a team of high-performing members ready to handle anything that comes their way. Doing this in the virtual world presents very real challenges mostly related to difficulties associated with building connections in an asynchronous environment. I wish there were one easy, readily identifiable answer, but there isn't. The best advice I can give is to put your team first, make the effort to connect, and allow them to connect with you.

All of the concepts I have discussed in this chapter may sound easy on paper, but in reality, they take a lot of time and effort to put into practice in the virtual world. Regardless of your level of commitment, regardless of how well you communicate and connect, there will still be failures. This is okay because to succeed, you must be willing to fail. My advice on this subject is to fail early and fail often, but always fail in a manner in which the recovery will move you forward. The only true failures in life are those from which we do not learn.

Finally, to do much of what I recommended, it requires effort and positive energy. You must love what you do so that you can be proud of your efforts and outcomes. I'll end with my favorite quote from one of my favorite all time athletes, Bernie Parent: "Enjoy what you are doing, or don't do it." I find this to be excellent life advice.

References:

Cimmarrusti, G. (2018, May). *Being a project manager is like being an artist, you have the different colored process streams combining into a work of art.* [Tweet]. Twitter. https://twitter.com/gcimmarrusti/status/99617569 4676705281?lang=en

Morris, P., & Hough, G. H. (1987). *The anatomy of major projects: A study of the reality of project management.* Wiley.

Nauman, S., Bhatti, S. H., Imam, H., & Khan, M. S. (2022). How servant leadership drives project team performance through collaborative culture and knowledge sharing. *Project Management Journal, 53*(1), 17–32. https://doi.org/10.1177/87569728211037777

Peek, S. (2023, November 7). Do results-only workplaces really work? *Business.com*. https://www.business.com/articles/do-results-only-workplaces-really-work/

Project Management Institute. [PMI]. (2013). *A guide to the project management body of knowledge* (PMBOK® Guide) (5th Edition ed.). Newtown Square, Pennsylvania: Project Management Institute, Inc.

Spears, L. (2010). Character and servant leadership: Ten characteristics of caring, effective leaders. *The Journal of Virtues & Leadership, 1(1),25-30.* https://www.regent.edu/journal/journal-of-virtues-leadership/character-and-servant-leadership-ten-characteristics-of-effective-caring-leaders/

Chapter Nine

Connection, Communication, and Influence in the Virtual Workplace

Catherine Mattiske

B usinesses and organizations that maintain a virtual workplace must consider how well remote workers feel connected to their team and whether they feel a sense of ownership over their work. In addition, leaders should periodically examine how effectively teams collaborate, and track project milestones using technology tools. While there are many benefits to maintaining a virtual workplace, some challenges must be addressed to ensure everyone feels connected and accountable.

In today's economy more and more businesses are using remote employees to save money on office space and overhead costs. Savvy businesses have also unlocked the potential of hiring from a global talent pool rather than their local community—a benefit that the virtual workplace model uniquely affords. While this trend has many benefits, it can also present challenges when maintaining a sense of community among team members or fostering a sense of ownership among employees.

Businesses and organizations that maintain a virtual workplace can be more successful than those that do not. However, strategies must be implemented to stay connected for this model to be effective. By utilizing communication tools like regular check-ins or video calls, remote workers can stay productive and feel like part of a team. The opportunities for high-performing teams to be influential and meet and exceed business goals are boundless in a virtual workplace environment.

The Importance of Connection, Communication, and Influence

As will be explored throughout the remainder of this chapter, three key drivers are essential to the continuous improvement of virtual human capital: *Connection*, *Communication*, and *Influence*. The following is a brief exploration of each one, and each one makes up an important part of the Genius Quotient Model, explored later in this chapter.

Connection is the foundation of virtual human capital, providing a platform to form relationships and build trust. Therefore, creating an atmosphere of connectedness among employees and organizations is essential to foster collaboration and growth. Through leveraging digital tools, such as video conferencing, social media platforms, and real-time chat systems, teams can more easily stay connected and communicate their needs.

Communication is the key to success in virtual workplaces. Virtual leaders must effectively communicate their mission, vision, and objectives with virtual team members to ensure everyone understands their expectations and how they can best contribute. Additionally, as virtual teams often lack a physical presence, virtual leaders must clearly communicate their message and actively engage virtual team members in decision-making.

Finally, virtual leaders must *Influence* virtual environments so virtual teams can get the most out of collaboration efforts. To be an effective virtual leader, one must possess active-listening, empathy, problem-solving, and delegation skills. With a robust virtual presence, leaders can effectively manage virtual teams and encourage them to reach their fullest potential by motivating, supporting, and inspiring team members.

Overall, virtual human capital is essential for companies looking to stay competitive in today's digital world. By implementing *Connection*, *Communication*, and *Influence* as three key drivers of virtual workplace success, leaders can ensure that virtual teams are more engaged and productive. With the right tools and strategies, virtual teams can collaborate effectively while achieving positive results.

Connection, Communication, and Influence in the Genius Quotient Model

The 'Genius Quotient' (Mattiske, 2021) refers to an individual's unique learning and communication preferences, while the 'Genius Zone' (Mattiske, 2021) is the optimal psychological state of flow where one does their best work and ultimately lives their best life. When groups of individuals come together, and each operates within their own Genius Zone, a powerful synergy emerges from the collaboration of complementary talents applied harmoniously.

The Genius Zone is a state of peak performance, creativity, and engagement in which people experience deep fulfilment, meaning, and impact by fully expressing their talents. In the Genius Zone, individuals are challenged with tasks that align with their innate abilities. In this state, they often report that they lose track of time because they are absorbed in an activity and thus produce their best work.

The Genius Quotient (GQ) Model (see Figure 1) provides a framework for teams to focus on productivity and motivation. It promotes the idea that being physically separated from one another does not have to be a hindrance if proper strategies are put in place. Teams can use this model to evaluate their current practices, develop new strategies, and measure their progress over time. Its focus on *learning*, *connection*, *communication*, and *influencing* (see Figure 1) helps teams achieve success in a remote working environment.

Additionally, the GQ Model helps teams build trust and sustain motivation by better understanding one another's strengths and weaknesses. This fosters better relationships among team members, leading to increased job satisfaction. Highly developed skills of connecting, communicating, and influencing encourage collaboration, creativity, problem-solving, and overall team growth.

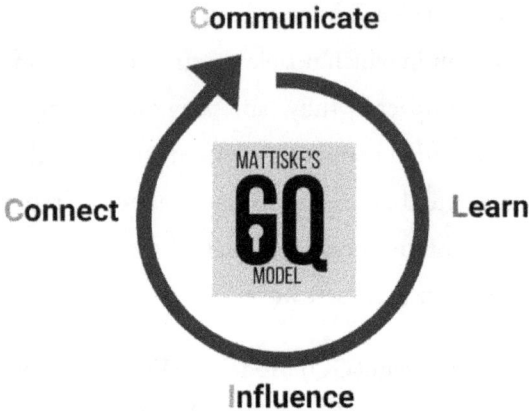

Figure 1 - Genius Quotient Model (Mattiske, 2021)

In three parts below, this chapter will explore three components of the GQ Model— *Connect*, *Communicate*, and *Influence*. The *Learn* component will be explored in Chapter 10.

Part 1 – Virtual Team Connection: Building Strong Relationships in a Remote Workforce

8 Anchors of a "Connect Mindset" for Virtual Leaders and Team Members

Successful virtual leaders and team members have a mindset to unite, embracing *Connect* as the basis for progress and productivity. The GQ Model is based on the principle of a unification mindset and provides eight anchors to help people develop their connect mindset.

These anchors serve as role models for others who wish to learn and build upon their own connect mindset. With an increased understanding of how to foster better collaboration through virtual connections, these anchor individuals and provide invaluable insight and guidance on leveraging the power of connection in today's modern virtual workplace. As such, they are truly inspiring others to reach for their potential and develop a second-to-none *Connect* mindset.

The eight *Connect* mindset anchors to help people get into their Genius Zone are:

    1. Use Names

2. Keep the Trust Account in Credit

3. Focus

4. Start Small: Ask "How Are You?"

5. Be Appreciative

6. Maintain Eye Connect

7. Crush Grumpy

8. Offer a Compliment

These anchors serve as tools for developing a strong *Connect* mindset. They challenge us to be open-minded, adaptive, and communicative in our virtual leadership and team roles, allowing us to create meaningful connections with those around us, regardless of physical distance. Each of the eight anchors will now be explored.

1. Use Names

Using names in virtual workplaces is a powerful tool for virtual leaders and team members. It helps build trust, connection, and camaraderie between people who may never have the chance to meet in person, enhancing communication, collaboration, and productivity.

2. Keep the Trust Account in Credit

For virtual leaders and team members, Stephen R. Covey's metaphor of the emotional bank account is especially pertinent in building trust in a virtual team (Covey, 2004). Virtual leaders make "deposits" into the trust account through honest communication and active listening. "Deposits" create a secure foundation of trust for virtual teams to work from, creating a sense of security, understanding, and respect. In addition, virtual leaders should respect all virtual team members during virtual conversations and meetings to avoid "withdrawals," and take the time to provide feedback and be consistent in their expectations.

Creating a trusted environment is essential for virtual leaders and team members to build connections in the virtual workplace. When people feel they can trust each other, it encourages them to open up and share their ideas, skills, and perspectives. This helps virtual teams become more collaborative, efficient, and productive.

Trust is also the foundation of psychological safety – an essential element in virtual team performance. Psychological safety allows leaders and virtual team members to take risks without fear of criticism or ridicule, allowing them to take on complex challenges and innovate, leading to new opportunities and increased productivity.

3. Focus

Focusing is essential for virtual leaders and team members to create connection and trust. It allows teams to stay organized, to stay on task, and to effectively use time and resources. Additionally, focusing helps to establish connection by enabling team members to work on tasks and objectives together without distractions. Finally, creating focus can help maintain the team's momentum and motivate them to achieve their goals.

4. Start Small: Ask "How Are You?"

Asking "How are you?" is an easy way to build relationships and foster a sense of connection between virtual team members. It serves as a simple reminder that, despite not being in the same geographical location, we still care about each other's well-being. It can create an atmosphere of care and empathy, which helps to build trust, collaboration, and understanding. Furthermore, it allows team members to share their feelings, experiences, and struggles in a safe space. This can lead to more open communication, productive problem-solving, and successful collaboration.

5. Be Appreciative

Showing appreciation is one of the most potent connection-building tools on virtual teams. Expressing gratitude for someone's efforts, dedication, and results helps create a sense of connection and inclusivity. In addition to making team members feel valued, appreciation can motivate good work and shape team dynamics.

6. Maintain Eye Contact

Maintaining eye contact during virtual meetings is a crucial part of connection and collaboration for teams. Turning cameras on during meetings and being aware of eye contact helps create an atmosphere of connection, trust, and understanding among team members, even when not physically present. In a virtual meeting, eye contact conveys an understanding of the other person's point of view, a visible cue that people are listening, and an appreciation for their perspective's value to the team. It also helps foster a sense of connection and unity among members, as they can better relate because of eye contact (Hansen, 2021).

7. Crush Grumpy

Avoiding, or crushing, grumpiness is essential in fostering connections among virtual team members. One of the most effective ways to combat grumpiness is through positive communication. Team members should be encouraged to communicate openly and honestly about their feelings, but constructively. This will create an environment that is conducive to connection and collaboration. Additionally, virtual teams might engage in team-building activities such as virtual happy hours, online game nights, and trivia competitions. These activities may help build connections and foster collaboration between team members who would otherwise remain strangers.

8. Offer a Compliment

As virtual teams become increasingly common, connection and collaboration are essential for success. A virtual leader offering compliments to team members can foster connection, build trust, and recognize individual contributions. Complimenting others makes team members feel appreciated and valued and helps create a productive working environment. Virtual leaders must take the initiative in complimenting others, reflecting that connection is a priority. Doing so will create an environment of connection and collaboration, helping to ensure success for the whole team.

Why Virtual Ownership Is Key to Success

Virtual ownership encourages connection between team members and a shared sense of responsibility for collective success. When everyone has a sense of ownership, it builds trust and connection that can be leveraged to drive results. When everyone takes responsibility for the team's success, it creates an environment of collaboration and accountability that can ultimately lead to greater efficiency and success. When team members feel connected, they are likelier to give their best effort and be committed to reaching their collective goals. By fostering a sense of virtual ownership, teams have the potential to become more productive and successful. Ultimately, creating an environment of connection and ownership among virtual teams is essential in driving collective success.

Recognize Individual Accomplishments in a Culture of Accountability

A virtual leader must foster connection and trust by regularly recognizing individual accomplishments and providing constructive feedback to drive performance. By creating a culture of accountability, team members will be more inclined to take ownership of their work and contribute at a higher level. In addition, the connection between virtual team members is strengthened when accomplishments are celebrated, and individual needs are addressed. Virtual leaders can recognize achievements on a team level and individually, which will help motivate and inspire team members to reach their fullest potential.

Harness the Power of Technology to Lead Virtual Teams

For virtual leaders and teams, it is crucial to understand the connection between technology and team effectiveness. Utilizing technology tools can help to ensure that projects stay on track and that all team members remain connected, even in a virtual setting. Virtual teams can collaborate effectively by leveraging technology tools such as online project management software and video conferencing platforms. Additionally, these tools can be used to track project milestones and progress accurately. Embracing the power of technology is vital to ensure that the team remains successful.

Virtual Leadership: Stay Connected Anywhere

The success of a virtual team relies on connection. As a virtual leader, take the initiative and create a connection between all team members. Utilize the tools available and foster connections with virtual team members. Doing so will equip them to succeed wherever they may be.

Staying connected should be at the top of the priority list. Implement strategies and systems to ensure the connection between team members. For example, consider setting up regular check-ins with colleagues and scheduling frequent video calls. This will help keep everyone informed and on the same page, enabling the team to stay productive and focused. Being proactive in creating connections and fostering collaboration is essential as a virtual leader. By doing so, you ensure your virtual team will be well-equipped to exceed expectations and reach their goals.

Conclusion

The influence of virtual leaders and individual team members on the group dynamics of a virtual team is paramount. Team leaders must know the potential challenges of working in a virtual environment and take proactive steps to ensure successful team communication. By fostering trust, providing clear expectations, utilizing the right communication strategies, and fostering a collaborative culture, virtual leaders can build strong relationships with their team members and create an effective working environment for the entire virtual team. With the right influence and leadership, virtual teams can maximize their productivity and create an environment where team members have a sense of connection, belonging, and ownership within the team.

❧〉〉 ┈ ◆ ┈ 〈〈❧

Part 2 – Virtual Communication: Crafting Clear Messages for Communicating Remotely

8 Anchors of a "Communication Mindset" for Virtual Leaders and Team Members

Part of a virtual leader's and virtual team member's success lies in creating a shared virtual "communication mindset" with the team to ensure that everyone is on the same page regarding virtual communication. Embracing *Communication* is paramount for team unity, workflow, and goal achievement.

The GQ Model is a powerful tool for virtual leaders and virtual team members to leverage to develop their *Communication* mindset. It consists of eight anchors which allow virtual leaders and virtual team members to hone their communication skills to collaborate, engage, and influence effectively.

The eight *Communication* mindset anchors to help people get into their Genius Zone are:

1. Focus

2. Ask High Impact Questions

3. Listen & Be Silent

4. Ask "What If?"

5. Dig Deeper

6. Yes . . . And

7. Smile

8. Take Notes

These mindset anchors provide a roadmap for virtual leaders and teams to emulate. By demonstrating effective communication, leaders ensure that virtual team members remain open-minded and adaptive. Through fostering an environment of mutual respect and understanding, leaders enable virtual team members to create meaningful communication, even when physical distance may be a hurdle.

1. Focus

Assertive communication with an absolute focus enables members to collaborate, build trust, and ultimately achieve team goals. Communication in virtual teams can be broken down into many components, such as virtual meetings, chats, document sharing, and team building. Virtual meetings allow teams to come together, focus, and discuss projects or make decisions.

2. Ask High Impact Questions

High Impact Questions (HIQs) are the virtual leader and team member communication tools to develop relationships, foster collaboration, and promote productive virtual work environments (Mattiske, 2022). HIQs are open-ended questions that require deep thinking, such as "What is the most important lesson you have learned during this project?" (as opposed to Low Impact Questions [LIQs], such as "How did the project go?" or "Did you learn much from the project?"). By asking and receiving thoughtful answers to HIQs, leaders and team members can form connections with each other and build trust. Additionally, HIQs can encourage virtual team members to think outside the box and develop creative solutions for team projects.

3. Listen & Be Silent

Being silent and listening are essential skills for virtual team members and leaders. In virtual teams, communication is vital for the team to be successful. The leader must listen carefully to understand the team's needs and objectives to lead them effectively. Likewise, virtual team members must listen when leaders give instructions and feedback, or it may lead to misunderstanding and confusion. By remembering that "listen" has the same letters as "silent," virtual team members can focus on engaging in active listening, which will help to ensure that everyone is engaged and on the same page (Mattiske, 2022).

4. Ask "What If?"

The "What if?" question can be a powerful tool for virtual leaders and team members. By asking "What if?" questions, virtual teams can explore various potential solutions and outcomes, encouraging creative thinking and collaboration. As virtual teams often face communication challenges due to limited face-to-face (in-person) interaction, the "What if?" question can help leaders and team members brainstorm ideas and get each other's perspectives and engage in creative business thinking. This type of team communication can help leaders and team members work together to make more informed decisions.

5. Dig Deeper

For virtual teams to be successful, leaders must strive to create an open and collaborative environment. This starts with team members actively engaging in virtual meetings. Digging deeper during virtual meetings by asking pertinent questions, offering insights from their experience, and engaging in a meaningful dialogue can strengthen communication between team members. Doing so can help leaders better understand the team's ideas, challenges, and progress while providing the team members with a deeper understanding of their role within the team.

6. Yes . . . and

Everyone can play an integral role in cultivating a positive communication environment. Using the phrase "Yes . . . and" in virtual meetings can foster an atmosphere of collaboration and collective problem-solving. It encourages team members to constructively add to one another's ideas and build upon existing conversations. By leveraging this phrase, leaders can actively engage team members in meaningful communication and create an environment of trust and cohesion. Furthermore, leaders can encourage team members to continue the discussion by building upon one another's ideas. Finally, this phrase can create an environment of collaboration and collective problem-solving.

7. Smile

Smiling during virtual meetings is an indispensable part of virtual communication. For a leader or team member, the ability to express emotion can help create a more friendly and comfortable environment. Smiling helps to build rapport, convey trustworthiness, and display engagement with the conversation. It also helps to create positive feelings and convey a sense of enthusiasm. Additionally, smiling during virtual meetings can help build relationships, foster collaboration, increase morale, and show respect for other team members.

8. Take Notes

For virtual leaders, taking notes during meetings is one of the best ways to ensure everyone remains on task and productive. The distance between virtual team members can make clarifying points or summarizing conversations challenging in virtual settings. Taking meeting notes helps leaders document issues, decisions, and action items discussed during meetings. It also helps team members stay on track when discussing complex topics and ensures that any decisions made are accurately recorded. In today's technology-driven world, various apps and software solutions are available to record a transcript of the meeting, which can be summarized and shared post-meeting.

❧ ⸱⸱◆⸱⸱ ❧

Communicate Effectively in a Virtual Workplace

Virtual communication requires leaders and team members to be mindful of their communication approach. Leaders must ensure that all communication is delivered professionally yet creatively, especially when communicating project expectations and team goals and providing feedback. Ensuring clear and direct communication is critical while remaining respectful and polite. Furthermore, communication should be structured in a way that is easy to understand and follow. Virtual leaders should ensure that communication is tailored to the individual needs of each team member and the team.

Improve Virtual Meeting Productivity with Active Listening

Active listening is a communication technique that involves paying close attention to what is being said during virtual meetings, allowing the speaker to know they are heard (Mattiske, 2022). This can be achieved through verbal cues such as nodding, repeating key points, and paraphrasing what was said. By actively listening during meetings, leaders encourage team members to participate and build trust between everyone.

Virtual leaders need to be mindful of communication protocols and etiquette. They should ask questions to get clarification, be aware of their nonverbal communication, and ensure that everyone has a chance to contribute to the discussion. Additionally, virtual team members should avoid multitasking and be present in the discussion by actively engaging with each other.

Create an Open Culture for Constructive Feedback and Idea Sharing

Creating a constructive feedback and idea-sharing culture in the virtual workplace can only function if the environment is based on trust and respect. For a virtual leader, setting communication expectations for the team is essential. Establishing communication parameters such as a regular time to check in and provide updates, setting response times for emails (if necessary), and having an open communication atmosphere encourages team members to have candid conversations.

Establishing a virtual environment where everyone feels comfortable expressing their ideas and opinions is crucial to developing an open culture. In addition, encouraging team members to ask questions or provide feedback, even if challenging, helps create an atmosphere of trust and respect.

To ensure that communication is constructive rather than confrontational, it is vital to allow team members to practice communication-related skills, including providing virtual communication workshops, offering communication tips, or role-playing communication scenarios.

Finally, virtual leaders should celebrate successes and be open to feedback from the team. Recognizing team members for their efforts when ideas are implemented and actively listening to feedback from the team will encourage an atmosphere of trust, creativity, and communication.

Create a Psychologically Safe and Trustworthy Virtual Space

Psychological safety, according to Edmondson, is "an absence of interpersonal fear," and when it is present, "people are able to speak up," which is a hallmark of communication and collaboration within virtual teams (Edmondson, 1999). Psychological safety refers to the level of trust and communication that is experienced among virtual team members and their leaders. When psychological safety is present, individuals are more likely to communicate openly and share their ideas and opinions without fear of judgment or reprisal. This encourages constructive communication and collaboration, allowing virtual teams to work more effectively toward their goals. Virtual leaders do not have the opportunity to manage by wandering around the office, so communication must be more direct, thoughtful, and pointed to maintain the connectivity of linking actions to the shared vision.

Conclusion

In conclusion, virtual communication is rapidly becoming the norm. With the proper knowledge and tools, virtual leaders and team members can leverage their communication skills to succeed. As a result, leading and collaborating has become an essential skill set for virtual teams. Furthermore, with clear communication, leaders can remain connected to their teams and build relationships with virtual communities. Virtual communication can then lead to increased productivity among remote teams and create a thriving virtual environment.

Part 3 – Virtual Influence: Mastering Effective Strategies to Inspire Change Virtually

8 Anchors of an "Influence Mindset" for Virtual Leaders and Team Members

Creating a robust virtual *Influence* mindset is essential for the success of both virtual leaders and their team members. An *Influence* mindset gives individuals the confidence to effectively reach out and impact people, ideas, and events. When an entire virtual team has a collective mindset around influencing others, they can work together in unison to bring their ideas and opinions to the forefront. In addition, the team's collective mindset allows them to think more strategically and identify opportunities for collaboration, rather than simply focusing on individual goals (Mattiske, 2022).

The GQ Model is a powerful tool for virtual leaders and virtual team members to leverage to develop their *Influence* mindset. It consists of eight anchors which allow virtual leaders and virtual team members to hone their influencing skills to be persuasive, collaborate, increase impact, and build positive working relationships.

The eight *Influence* mindset anchors to help people get into their Genius Zone are:

1. Be a Sleuth

2. Show Value

3. Give

4. Ask "Will You . . . ?"

5. Find Others

6. Find Common Ground

7. Be Unique

8. Yes, Yes, Yes

These mindset anchors provide guidance and set an example for virtual leaders and teams to emulate. By demonstrating effective influence, virtual leaders and teams remain calm under pressure and maintain a professional demeanor to influence those around them effectively.

1. Be a Sleuth

Robert Cialdini speaks of Sleuths, Bunglers, and Smugglers when illustrating influence (Cialdini, 2009). The Sleuth strategically plans and seeks out opportunities to influence; the Bungler relies on ineffective or counterproductive methods; and the Smuggler uses unethical tactics in a manipulative manner. Ultimately, the Sleuth succeeds where the others fail by employing ethical strategies and careful planning to create positive outcomes for all involved.

2. Show Value

Increasing influence in a virtual workspace can be done by demonstrating value, because people are more likely to listen and respond positively to those with the most to offer. It is important to note that demonstrating value does not simply mean having the right qualifications or expertise but showing up and contributing to the space in meaningful ways—for example, offering advice or expertise on a particular topic, taking the lead on projects, or offering to help out a colleague. These activities demonstrate value and importance and will increase influence in the virtual workspace.

3. Give

One of the most effective ways to increase influence in the virtual workplace is through giving. When people act with generosity and give their time, resources, knowledge, and connections to help their peers, they create deeper relationships, increase morale, and promote camaraderie, which can lead to increased influence (Cialdini, 2009). In addition, by giving, virtual leaders and team members demonstrate that they are valuable assets to the company and worthy of respect. Giving benefits the recipient and the giver, who can reap the rewards of having a more robust professional network and an enhanced reputation for generosity.

4. Ask "Will You...?"

Asking "Will you . . . ?" can be a powerful way to increase one's influence in the virtual workplace. The phrase "Will you . . .?" is a form of language that can bring others into the conversation and promote engagement with the task at hand. Using this phrase, one can create an environment of trust and collaboration essential for successful virtual workplace relationships. This is because such an inquiry encourages employees to take ownership of outcomes, giving them a sense of responsibility and control. Furthermore, it shows that one is interested in the input of others and respects their opinions.

5. Find Others

By being part of a group, individuals can leverage the collective power of their peers and combine forces to achieve common objectives. Groups in the virtual workspace also provide a platform for knowledge sharing and collaboration. By working together, members of the same virtual group can build stronger relationships, gain insights into industry trends, and create more effective campaigns. Additionally, working with like-minded peers offers an excellent opportunity to learn from others and share new perspectives and ideas (Cohen, 1984). As such, being part of a cohesive group in the virtual workspace can significantly boost an individual's influence and help them to reach their goals.

6. Find Common Ground

Finding common ground with a diverse virtual team is essential to increase influence in the virtual workplace. By understanding each other's cultural backgrounds, values, and beliefs, virtual team members can more easily identify areas of agreement. This shared understanding can lead to increased collaboration and cooperation between the different members of the virtual team and ultimately result in more effective problem-solving. Additionally, by considering each other's unique perspectives and strengths, virtual teams can better identify and capitalize on opportunities to maximize their collective influence. As a result, teams are capable of producing more robust results in the virtual workplace.

7. Be Unique

Being unique and standing out in the virtual workplace can significantly increase one's influence. This is because when someone stands out, they are seen as a leader, and people will look to them for guidance and advice. Furthermore, when someone is seen as a leader, they can shape the conversation and be a role model for other people. Additionally, as one stands out from the crowd, they are more likely to be seen as an expert in their field, increasing their influence. Finally, standing out from the crowd can boost one's confidence and make them more likely to take on new challenges, leading to increased influence.

8. Yes, Yes, Yes

Asking a question where someone answers "yes" triggers a pattern where they are more likely to continue agreeing (Fisher & Ury, 2012). Asking consecutive questions where the answers are all "yes" sparks Cialdini's 'commitment and consistency' principle. This is when people are more likely to be consistent in their behavior once they have made a public commitment (Cialdini, 2009). For example, asking the question, "Is a week enough time to do the report?" to which the answer is "Yes," can be followed by, "Shall we meet at 2 p.m. Tuesday?" to which the answer is "Yes." And then, "Will you prepare a short presentation for the team showing the report next Tuesday?" to which the answer is "Yes." (Note the use of the "Will you . . . ?" question referenced above.) The "3 Yeses" technique is a compelling influence method for greater cooperation, commitment, trust, and engagement (Mattiske, 2022).

❖ ⋯ ✦ ⋯ ❖

Creative Problem-Solving for the Virtual Workplace

In the virtual workplace, creative problem-solving is essential for finding equitable and respectful solutions. Creative problem-solving encourages participants to think outside the box, explore different perspectives, and use their imagination to develop innovative solutions (Mattiske, 2022). Practicing creative problem-solving skills in the virtual workplace is vital to cultivate an open and creative mindset. This includes avoiding assumptions about the problem and being open to different ideas and solutions. It is also essential to involve all participants in the process by encouraging them to contribute their ideas, opinions, and solutions. Acknowledging each person's unique perspective makes it possible to find a solution that works for everyone.

Amplify Voices within the Virtual Workplace

In the virtual workplace, influence and power dynamics can be challenging to navigate. Ensuring that underrepresented voices are heard is essential to create a more equitable and productive workplace. One way to achieve this is by creating dialogue space and increasing underrepresented groups' representation in decision-making roles (Mattiske, 2020).

Virtual leaders can influence the team dynamic by actively seeking input from their virtual team members and recognizing when particular perspectives have not been included. More diversity in decision-making roles can help ensure that all opinions are considered and lead to better overall decisions.

Create a Transparent and Trusting Workplace That Encourages Innovation

Creating a workplace of transparency and trust is one of the most potent ways to influence virtual team members and unlock their creative potential and unbounded influence across the organization and external groups.

This type of environment requires virtual leaders to be open and honest about the team's goals, processes, and vision. Leaders should strive to maintain an environment of trust by encouraging team members to voice their opinions and take risks. A supportive atmosphere where everyone is held accountable for their decisions is essential for fostering an innovative environment (Mattiske, 2020).

Transparency and trust can also be encouraged by creating a culture of open communication in which team members feel comfortable sharing their ideas and offering constructive feedback. It is also vital to ensure that team members understand the implications of failure and the rewards of success. This encourages bold thinking and allows virtual teams to push beyond their comfort zones and develop creative solutions.

Generate Ideas and Collaborate in a Virtual Space

As we move further into the virtual work environment being the norm, it is crucial to recognize how influence can be used creatively and collaboratively. The virtual leader is responsible for creating an understanding of influence and developing trust among team members. Utilizing influence effectively can help inspire idea generation and promote collaboration with diverse perspectives, and challenge the status quo to enable new ideas to surface and solve problems in ways that may not initially come to mind.

One way to influence virtually is by using tools and technology that can help foster creativity, such as brainstorming, affinity mapping, and online whiteboarding tools. Brainstorming helps to generate different ideas and solutions, while affinity mapping can help structure and organize them. With online whiteboarding tools, team members can add their perspectives and insights in one place for everyone to see and interact with, simultaneously driving collaboration and supercharged communication.

Conclusion

In conclusion, influence is a powerful tool for virtual leaders and team members. It can be used to inspire change and create positive outcomes. Virtual influence requires thoughtful consideration and implementation of effective strategies, such as leveraging relationships, technology, and resources to create an impactful influence. When virtual leaders and team members understand the elements of influence and how to apply them, influence can be a powerful tool for inspiring change, and a highly effective strategy for motivating and inspiring team members.

References

Cialdini, R. B. (2009). *Influence: The psychology of persuasion.* HarperCollins US.

Cohen, R. J. (1984). Influence: How and why people agree to things. *Psychology & Marketing, 1,* 139-140. https://onlinelibrary.wiley.com/doi/abs/10.1002/mar.4220010317

Covey, S. (2004). *The 7 habits of highly effective people: Restoring the character ethic (Rev. ed.).* Free Press.

Edmondson, A. (1999). Psychological safety and learning behavior in work teams. *Administrative Science Quarterly, 44*(2), 350–383. https://doi.org/10.2307/2666999.

Fisher, R., & Ury, W. (2012). *Getting to yes: Negotiating an agreement without giving in.* Century.

Hansen, J. (2021). *Look me in the eye: Using video to build relationships with customers, partners and teams.* Acting for Sales, LLC.

Mattiske, C. (2022). *Creative business thinking: Developing the skills for thinking outside the box.* Sydney: TPC - The Performance Company Pty Limited.

Mattiske, C. (2022). *Influencing for opportunity: Identify and maximize ways to influence (Learning Short-Take).* Sydney: TPC - The Performance Company Pty Limited.

Mattiske, C. (2020). *Leading virtual teams: Managing from a distance during the Coronavirus.* Sydney: TPC - The Performance Company Pty Limited.

Mattiske, C. (2022). *Listen & be listened to.* Sydney, Australia: TPC - The Performance Company Pty Limited.

Mattiske, C. (2021). *Unlock inner genius: Power your path to extraordinary success.* Sydney: TPC - The Performance Company Pty Limited.

Section VI – Continuous Improvement

Chapter Ten

The Value of a Growth Mindset for Continuous Improvement in a Virtual Workplace

Catherine Mattiske

To maintain a healthy balance between in-office and virtual work, continuous improvement of team members and leaders is critical. In the current business landscape, many workers are completing their tasks remotely. This shift has brought about new trends, challenges, and issues that organizations must account for to succeed. Although organizations must create a space for employees to express their thoughts, ideas, and concerns virtually, simply having a platform is not enough. Strong connections in a dynamic environment driven by continuous improvement with the team at all organizational levels ensure better performance when working virtually.

To further optimize virtual work strategies and practices, building a solid foundation of trust with workers will be paramount in allowing any organization's booming growth. By understanding the importance of continuous improvement in a virtual workplace, organizations can create an environment conducive to success.

One key driver is essential to continuous improvement for team members: *learning*. This is one concept of the Genius Quotient Model, introduced in the previous chapter.

The Genius Quotient Model

Introduced in the previous chapter, the "Genius Quotient" (Mattiske, 2021) is a concept gaining traction among individuals, teams, and leadership structures as they face the ongoing issues, trends, and challenges virtual work presents. This model provides the strategies and practices to sustain and optimize virtual work, allowing individual team members to operate more effectively while doing their part in creating a solid group dynamic. As stated in chapter 9, teams can use the Genius Quotient (GQ) Model (see Figure 1) to evaluate their current practices, develop new strategies, and measure their progress over time. Its focus on *learning*, *connection*, *communication*, and *influencing* helps teams achieve success in a remote working environment.

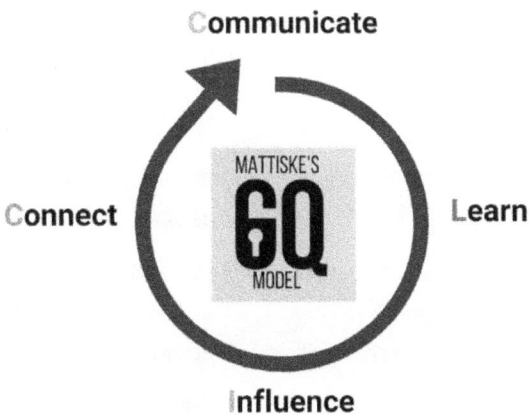

Figure 1 – Genius Quotient Model (Mattiske, 2021)

In addition, the Genius Quotient's integrated approach ensures that all the critical elements addressing present issues receive attention simultaneously. It also leads to greater connection with peers and leaders, optimal communication among diverse groups, increased potential to influence at all levels of the organization, and an ever-changing environment with achievable goals and increased accountability.

Ultimately, the GQ Model provides a framework for teams that allows them to become more productive and motivated in this new era of working remotely. In chapter 9, we explored the concepts of *Connect, Communicate*, and *Influence* in the GQ Model. This chapter will explore the last component—*Learn*, which focuses on harnessing a growth mindset for leaders and team members.

The Missing Link to Successful Virtual Leadership – A Growth Mindset

Developing a growth mindset is critical for workplace learning in the virtual environment and to ensure continuous improvement. Leaders and team members must understand that there is an opportunity to learn something new every day and be willing to take risks by trying new things, even if they do not always work out. With a growth mindset, employees are motivated to acquire knowledge and skills and are not discouraged by failures or mistakes. Instead, they recognize that challenges and mistakes provide an opportunity to learn, grow, and develop.

A growth mindset is the cornerstone of effective virtual leadership. Leaders must develop a growth mindset to equip their team members with the necessary skills and self-awareness to complete tasks while effectively working remotely. This shift in thinking allows leaders and team members to make decisions quickly and confidently, take ownership of tasks, and maximize their productivity in a virtual setting. As such, leaders must cultivate an effective growth mindset for problem-solving virtual challenges within the team.

Promoting Continuous Improvement through Growth Mindset and Effective Virtual Leadership

Having a growth mindset and cultivating an effective virtual leadership environment are instrumental for continuous improvement. By embracing a growth mindset, employees can be more open to feedback and push themselves to learn new skills even when the task is difficult or unfamiliar. With this ongoing development of knowledge, employees will have the confidence to take on future challenges with optimism, which in turn promotes continuous improvement and helps the team become more successful.

Leaders must also foster an open environment that encourages employees to ask questions, share ideas, and work together to achieve goals. By fostering this type of growth-oriented workplace, leaders can create a culture of continuous improvement where everyone is learning, growing, and contributing toward team success.

Leaders should foster open communication within their team that encourages learning and development by actively seeking feedback from each member and acknowledging successes (Mattiske, 2022). They should also guide how to tackle remote work issues such as time management or technical difficulties. By focusing on creating an environment of continuous learning, leader and team members alike will be better equipped to handle the challenges that come with virtual leadership.

To successfully lead a team remotely, leaders must embrace growth mindset practices and foster an atmosphere of creativity, innovation, and collaboration. Only by doing this can leaders ensure their teams are working to their full potential and reaching their goals while working virtually.

8 Anchors of a Growth Mindset For Virtual Leaders and Team Members

Successful people have a growth mindset, embracing *Learn* as the foundation for growth and success. The GQ Model is based on the principle of a growth mindset, and the *Learn* component of the model provides eight anchors to help people develop their growth mindset.

These anchors focus on learning from others who display a vibrant growth mindset. In addition, these individuals demonstrate qualities that can be adopted by those wishing to develop and strengthen their growth mindset through virtual leadership and team development.

The eight growth mindset anchors are:

1. Get Support

2. Be Decisive

3. Exhibit Consistency

4. Show up!

5. Smash Negativity

6. Take Risks

7. Embrace Positive Energy

8. Go Slow

By developing growth mindset anchors, virtual leaders and team members can ensure they are ready to embrace growth mindset principles and *Learn*. This will help them to be more successful in their roles and have better outcomes for the growth of their teams. With a growth mindset, virtual leaders and team members can ensure that growth opportunities are maximized, and that growth is accelerated. This enables success to be achieved more sustainably by creating an environment of growth and development. The growth mindset and *Learn* anchors help virtual leaders and teams to reach their full potential. Each of the eight growth mindset anchors will now be explained.

1. Get Support

Once virtual leaders and team members have adopted a growth mindset to identify the aspects of their organization that need change, it is essential to get support from individuals who understand and can help foster continuous improvement. With a growth mindset in place, leaders and team members can embrace change as an opportunity for growth and success rather than something to be feared or avoided. Continuous improvement and a commitment to learning are key to long-term success in the ever-evolving virtual environment.

A leader's mindset is incredibly influential and can be a powerful motivator for other team members. Therefore, it is essential to identify mentors, coaches, or colleagues who possess a virtual growth mindset that can help guide and motivate the team to success. By tapping into the expertise of these individuals, leaders and team members will gain the necessary skills and resources to become successful. Additionally, they will be more likely to stay motivated while working in a virtual environment as someone is available who understands the challenges being faced. Finally, building a support system of like-minded individuals, leaders, and team members can develop the skills and strategies they need to succeed in their virtual roles.

When working in a virtual environment, it is essential to share ideas with other leaders and team members to further build on what has been established. As such, they should connect with others with the same virtual growth mindset. Doing so will help them stay focused on their personal trajectories and goals while taking advantage of their peers' collective experiences.

Forming relationships with leaders and team members within the virtual environment fosters collaboration and knowledge sharing, ultimately leading to greater success in handling the challenges of this setting.

Overall, leaders and team members must be willing to invest time in themselves and their peers to create a successful virtual growth mindset that can take them far in their respective virtual roles. Leaders and team members can develop the skills and knowledge needed to succeed in a virtual environment by getting the necessary support from peers and mentors. Additionally, they should form relationships with like-minded leaders and team members, which will help foster collaboration and growth. Doing so will ensure leaders and team members have the necessary resources to build a thriving virtual growth mindset.

2. Be Decisive

Decisiveness is the cornerstone of leading a successful virtual team. As leaders and team members, we must be able to make decisions quickly and effectively in order to drive progress. We must have an open mindset toward our ideas and their potential outcomes; this will ensure that our previous assumptions or biases do not hold us back. Additionally, we must be comfortable in taking calculated risks; this will facilitate innovation, agility, and progress.

Leaders must also communicate effectively with their team members so everyone is on the same page when making decisions. Leaders should establish clear communication channels between themselves and their team members to understand each other's perspectives and listen to each other's thoughts (Mattiske, 2022). This will allow all stakeholders to be involved rather than making decisions in a vacuum.

Furthermore, leaders must ensure that decision-making processes are transparent and involve all stakeholders. This will promote collaboration, trust, and accountability within the team. Finally, leaders must set clear expectations so that team members know what is expected of them and can provide input confidently.

By leveraging a virtual growth mindset, leaders and team members alike can make decisions quickly and effectively, fostering a culture of innovation, agility, and progress.

3. Exhibit Consistency

To foster a virtual growth mindset, leaders and team members need to exhibit consistency. Leaders should support the development of their team by providing guidance and direction on how they can progress toward their goals. They must remain consistent in their expectations so that their team understands what is expected of them. Additionally, the leader should communicate changes or updates to the team so everyone is on the same page.

Team members should also strive to maintain consistent focus and dedication toward their work, even when working remotely. This can be done by setting personal goals and objectives that serve as motivators throughout the day and creating routines that help keep them on track. Additionally, team members should take the initiative to stay in touch with their leader and fellow colleagues to consistently stay up to date on any changes or updates that could influence their work.

By exhibiting consistency, virtual leaders and team members can foster a growth mindset in their organization and help drive positive change within their teams. They can create an environment of growth and development by setting expectations, providing clear communication, and taking the initiative. This will help build a positive culture of collaboration and success within the organization.

4. Show Up!

Showing up is much more than being present. It is about having a growth mindset, where one is open to embracing new ideas, learning from mistakes, and striving for improvement.

Leaders and team members who show up for virtual meetings with a growth mindset are essential in creating a dynamic, productive work environment. In addition, with technology increasingly becoming the primary means of communication, demonstrating an openness to learning and improving is essential for companies to stay competitive.

The importance of being prepared, present, and actively working in a virtual environment cannot be overstated.

- **Leaders** should focus on setting clear expectations and communicating regularly with their teams. This will ensure a clear understanding of deadlines and objectives and keep everyone on the same page. Additionally, leaders should know their team members' work styles to best collaborate during virtual meetings.

- **Team members** should come prepared by accessing necessary documents, staying focused on tasks, and being open to constructive feedback. They should also maintain an organized workspace with minimal visual distractions to ensure maximum focus. Having cameras and microphones on during virtual meetings creates a shared space that simulates the experience of being together in person. This allows participants to communicate more naturally and make meaningful connections with each other even when working remotely.

By fostering an environment that encourages active participation and engagement, that is, "showing up," leaders can help their teams stay motivated and effective in a virtual setting. With the right leader guiding the way, combined with camera-on culture, team members can have productive conversations and come to solutions more quickly—ultimately leading to improved workflows and project outcomes.

5. Smash Negativity

Developing a growth mindset is an essential factor in being personally and professionally successful. Smashing negativity can help foster the growth of this mindset. By recognizing and reframing negative thoughts and behaviors, leaders can create a positive working environment where growth is encouraged.

For virtual team members, smashing negativity can result in improved performance. Reframing negative thoughts helps individuals better understand their own growth and potential. Furthermore, it can help virtual team members recognize their own growth and the growth of others in the organization.

6. Take Risks

Taking risks is an integral part of the growth mindset, and virtual leaders have the unique opportunity to encourage risk-taking in their virtual team members. Encouraging risk-taking is a way to foster growth and creativity, as well as a growth mindset. For virtual leaders, this means taking their team members out of their comfort zones to explore new ideas and approaches.

This could involve sharing innovative ideas, trying different tasks or projects, or leading team members through a growth mindset technique like brainstorming. It could also allow team members to take on greater responsibility and try out new roles or assignments. By taking risks and trying new things, virtual team members can learn, grow, and develop growth mindset skills.

7. Embrace Positive Energy

Embracing positive energy is a crucial concept for a growth mindset and virtual teams. It allows leaders to create an atmosphere of growth and collaboration, motivating virtual team members to reach higher levels of excellence.

It helps virtual teams to stay connected and motivated no matter what the challenges may be. It allows virtual leaders to create a culture of growth and collaboration within their virtual teams, leading to increased productivity, greater efficiency, and improved results. Positive energy can also help virtual team members to develop a growth mindset, enabling them to think beyond their current reality and reach for higher levels of excellence. By embracing positive energy, a growth mindset can become a reality, and virtual teams will be better prepared to tackle any challenge that comes their way. In addition, this type of growth mindset encourages creativity and innovation, resulting in a more successful virtual team. Ultimately, embracing positive energy enables virtual teams to take their performance to the next level.

8. Go Slow

Going slow helps build a growth mindset in virtual leaders and team members. It encourages taking the time to understand the problem and develop strategies to solve it rather than jumping to conclusions or acting impulsively. Understanding a problem and developing a plan to address it is more conducive to growth than rushing to a solution.

The anchor of Going Slow also allows virtual leaders and team members to practice mindfulness by giving them the time to reflect on their growth, as well as the growth of others. With this kind of reflection, virtual leaders and team members can better identify areas where growth is needed and find ways to foster growth throughout their team. By slowing down and reflecting, leaders and team members can cultivate a growth mindset and create an environment that fosters growth for everyone.

Summary – 8 Anchors of a Virtual Growth Mindset

Developing a growth mindset for problem-solving virtual challenges is integral for successful virtual leadership. With this in mind, leaders should cultivate an effective growth mindset for problem-solving remote work issues within their team.

Tailor Strategies to Virtual Team Preferences

When working with virtual teams, it is essential to understand how team members prefer to learn and collaborate. This includes considering individual preferences for communication tools, workspace, and how they prefer to learn and communicate. For example, some team members may prefer meetings, while others may prefer asynchronous forms of communication, such as email. Additionally, team members may have different preferences regarding their workspace; some might prefer a quiet home office environment, while others may be more productive in a shared office space or a busy, noisy environment like their local café. By understanding virtual team members' learning preferences and tailoring strategies accordingly to foster continuous improvement, growth mindset, and learning agility, virtual teams are better equipped to work together effectively and efficiently to achieve their goals.

Use Team Learning Preferences to Prepare for a Virtual Work Environment

When virtual teams come together to work and collaborate, it is essential to assess the various learning preferences of the team. Everyone has different strengths, abilities, and challenges that must be considered. By understanding each team member's learning preferences, virtual teams can make thoughtful decisions about engaging with one another in virtual environments.

To ensure a thriving virtual working environment for all team members, start by assessing what works best for each member. This could include preferred communication methods such as email or chat platforms, video conferencing tools like Zoom or Skype, or interactive virtual whiteboard sessions. Once leaders and team members know everyone's preferences and needs, they can create strategies to support each team member and help them maximize their working experience.

Understanding the learning preferences of virtual team members can also help tailor strategies for success. "Brain fuel" describes individuals' preference for taking in information—via their five senses. For instance, virtual team members who prefer visual learning methods could benefit from referencing documents and viewing diagrams and presentations during virtual meetings instead of relying solely on verbal communication. As well, if virtual team members prefer to learn by doing, providing opportunities for hands-on activities can help facilitate a thriving team environment. Lastly, incorporating engaging group discussions into meetings will be vital for those who prefer to take in information via talking and listening.

Additionally, it is crucial to consider the challenges that virtual teams may face regarding learning preferences. This could include language barriers, cultural differences, or even technology-related issues. By understanding these challenges and adjusting accordingly, virtual teams can create an environment where everyone feels comfortable participating in tasks and activities.

Virtual teams can ensure successful collaboration and productivity in virtual settings by preparing for virtual work environments with a greater focus on learning preferences. As virtual work becomes increasingly prevalent, understanding how best to accommodate different learning preferences is integral for any successful virtual team. With thoughtful strategies that support all virtual team members, virtual work environments can be effectively managed, and successful results can be achieved.

The Benefits of Leadership Flexibility for Continuous Improvement and Virtual Teams

Leadership flexibility is key to continuous improvement, and this means leaders must adopt a growth mindset. Leaders should be open to new ideas, actively seek out innovative solutions, and work with their teams to identify areas for improvement.

By fostering an environment of open communication, collaboration, and respect, virtual team members will feel empowered to take initiative on tasks and projects. Leaders should also strive to provide their teams with the resources and support they need to make meaningful changes and reach their goals.

With leadership flexibility, organizations can foster an environment of continuous improvement and become more agile, productive, and successful in a constantly changing landscape. By investing in initiatives such as employee education, training programs, and virtual team technology, leaders can create an environment of growth and opportunity for their teams.

Ultimately, with a flexible leadership style, virtual teams can be utilized to reach targets and deadlines while encouraging greater organizational flexibility effectively. In this way, virtual teams become essential tools that enable organizations to adapt quickly to changing conditions and remain competitive in today's dynamic business environment.

Through leadership flexibility, organizations can leverage virtual teams to reach their goals and unlock the full potential of their employees. Ultimately, this can lead to productivity and *tremendous* success for the organization.

Leveraging the Power of Teamwork in a Virtual Setting

Creating a virtual workspace where everyone feels included and safe is essential for fostering productive collaboration. By recognizing cultural differences and individual needs, addressing microaggressions, and focusing on each team member's Genius Zone (a state of peak performance in which people experience deep fulfilment, as introduced in the previous chapter) and the synergy from their Collective Genius Zone, teams can create an environment of understanding and appreciation (Mattiske, 2022).

Leaders must have a growth mindset to recognize that every member has something unique to contribute to leverage their individual strengths while also leveraging the power of teamwork within their Collective Genius Zone. This leads to continuous improvement both individually and across the entire team.

Team members should be encouraged to express their ideas and opinions without fear and to bring their unique perspectives to the virtual workspace. This can be achieved by building a culture of respect and openness, where everyone feels welcomed and safe to contribute.

Leaders should take an active role in promoting inclusion across virtual teams by creating a shared understanding of team values, setting clear expectations around virtual etiquette (including topics such as appropriate language and communication methods), and establishing mechanisms for conflict resolution.

By embracing virtual diversity, teams will be better equipped to identify areas of improvement and use their Collective Genius Zones as a source of innovation. Through these steps, virtual teams can create an environment that drives positive results, embraces continuous improvement, while recognizing cultural differences and individual needs. The following are ten strategies for creating a safe and inclusive workspace by continuously improving cultural awareness:

1. Acknowledge that everyone has a different background and life experience.

2. Be aware of personal biases and assumptions.

3. Make an effort to learn about the cultures of coworkers.

4. Respect the personal space of coworkers and avoid invading their space without permission.

5. Avoid making assumptions about what someone

does or does not know based on their cultural background.

6. Use inclusive language when communicating with coworkers, avoiding terms that may be offensive or exclusionary.

7. Be aware of common cultural stereotypes and avoid perpetuating them in the workplace.

8. If someone is being treated unfairly or disrespectfully, speak up and stand up for them.

9. Seek out opportunities to celebrate the cultural diversity of the workplace.

10. Support policies and initiatives that promote a safe and inclusive workplace for all employees.

❖❖ · ·❖· ·❖❖

Optimizing Leadership Productivity and Team Performance When Working Virtually

Working in a virtual environment can be challenging, especially when productivity and focus are paramount. Therefore, leaders must understand how to make the most of the situation and ensure their team is productive while working remotely. Here are some tips on how to boost productivity and maintain focus while leading a virtual team:

1. **Foster a Growth Mindset**. Encouraging team members to stay positive, learn from mistakes, and focus on continuous improvement will create an environment of growth and productivity. Leaders should foster an attitude of learning and growth while providing the necessary resources for success in a virtual setting.

2. **Prioritize Continuous Improvement**. Continuously assess each team member's progress and provide feedback often so everyone is on track with their goals. Additionally, encouraging regular conversations about tasks and objectives makes it easier for leaders to identify areas needing improvement as well as individual strengths that can be leveraged for better results.

3. **Utilize Productivity Tools**. Leveraging technology and tools is essential for successful remote work environments. Identifying and making use of productivity tools such as video conferencing, online chat platforms, project management systems, and task-tracking apps can help keep everyone connected

and working together effectively.

4. **Set Clear Expectations**. Setting clear expectations for team members will ensure that tasks are completed in a timely manner. Leaders should make sure the team understands their objectives and knows what is expected of them to avoid confusion or delays.

5. **Promote Open Communication**. Having open lines of communication between team members helps build trust while encouraging collaboration on projects quickly. Frequent check-ins also help keep teams together and productive in the virtual environment.

6. **Be Available**. Leader availability is critical for virtual teams to succeed in completing their tasks efficiently and on time. Leaders must remain accessible to the team to provide guidance and direction, and to help resolve conflicts quickly when needed.

By following these tips, leaders can ensure that their virtual teams are able to focus on the task at hand while creating a positive work culture conducive to continuous learning and improvement. With effective leadership, virtual teams will be better equipped for success in the virtual workplace.

⟪⟫ ··· ◆ ··· ⟪⟫

Nine Practical Ways for Virtual Team Members to Improve Performance

The modern workplace is becoming increasingly virtual, and it is crucial that virtual team members develop effective methods to assess their work performance to maintain high productivity levels. Here are nine practical ways virtual team members can use to assess their performance and make necessary improvements (Mattiske, 2020).

1. **Set realistic goals.** Virtual team members should set realistic goals that focus on consistent growth and improvement. These goals should be achievable yet challenging to motivate the team member to strive for success over time.

2. **Use a continuous improvement mindset**. Virtual team members should adopt a continuous improvement attitude when assessing their performance, constantly evaluating successes and failures, and using the lessons learned to improve their performance over time.

3. **Regularly assess virtual tasks.** A virtual team member should evaluate their virtual tasks regularly to ensure they are correctly completed on time, and in the most cost-efficient manner possible while minimizing any potentially costly mistakes.

4. **Maintain cohesive virtual teams.** A virtual team member should pay attention to how well their teammates work together and strive to maintain a healthy level of collaboration. This will help maximize the productivity of each individual and the entire team.

5. **Monitor virtual communication.** Virtual team members should assess their communication with fellow virtual team members and ensure it is effective enough to achieve collective goals efficiently and effectively.

6. **Provide timely virtual feedback.** Virtual team members should provide feedback to each other regularly, helping identify areas for improvement and building a collective ability to self-correct tasks.

7. **Track virtual progress.** A virtual team member should maintain regular records of their own progress to ensure that tasks are completed on time

and with the most efficient use of resources.

8. **Use appropriate tools and technologies.** Virtual team members should use the right tools and technologies when completing their tasks; this requires evaluating which tools best suit their needs to optimize performance.

9. **Stay motivated and engaged.** Finally, virtual team members must remain motivated and engaged during all aspects of their work, as this will help them reach their goals more efficiently.

By utilizing these nine methods of virtual self-improvement, virtual team members can effectively assess their work performance, identify areas for improvement, and ensure that virtual tasks are completed in the most efficient manner possible. With a growth mindset and a focus on continuous improvement, as well as learning from mistakes and employing appropriate tools, team members can reach their goals and consistently maintain high levels of virtual work performance.

Conclusion

In conclusion, a virtual work environment presents unique opportunities to foster collaboration, communication, and learning. By recognizing the power of virtual collaboration, virtual teams can become more effective and successful.

Virtual leaders should strive to create a continuous improvement mindset by encouraging open dialogue between team members and providing an environment that supports growth and learning. They should also emphasize the importance of a continuous improvement approach by focusing on developing strong relationships with team members and promoting a culture of shared knowledge among them. In addition, leaders should provide team members with the resources needed to develop their skills and knowledge, allowing them to reach their full potential.

Through activities such as virtual meetings or training sessions, virtual teams can further develop their skills while creating an atmosphere of mutual respect and trust. Ultimately, when continuous improvement is encouraged within a supportive learning environment, it can lead to great success for the entire team.

References

Mattiske, C. (2020). *Leading virtual teams: Managing from a distance during the Coronavirus.* Sydney: TPC - The Performance Company Pty Limited.

Mattiske, C. (2021). *Unlock inner genius: Power your path to extraordinary success.* Sydney: TPC - The Performance Company Pty Limited.

Mattiske, C. (2022). *Creative business thinking: Developing the skills for thinking outside the box.* Sydney: TPC - The Performance Company Pty Limited.

Mattiske, C. (2022). *Influencing for opportunity: Identify and maximize ways to influence (Learning Short-Take).* Sydney: TPC - The Performance Company Pty Limited.

Mattiske, C. (2022). *Listen & be listened to.* Sydney, Australia: TPC - The Performance Company Pty Limited.

Chapter Eleven

Conclusion: Navigating the Future of Remote Work – Understanding the Challenges and Opportunities

Cristina Imre

"I imagine a world where you work from home, a coffee shop, a coworking space, next to a beach, or wherever you want, and the only 'must' is a stable internet connection.

What would it feel like to know this is your future" (Imre, 2018)?

Five years ago, I wrote these words, which now seem almost archaic. Changes have been rapid, and the COVID-19 pandemic only accelerated the widespread adoption of remote working. It has the potential to be a liberating force, giving people access to opportunities they may have otherwise been denied.

When discriminatory tendencies are removed from the equation, remote work can become an incredibly powerful equalizing force. It has the potential to open up opportunities for people who may otherwise have been denied access to them.

Moreover, the remote work economy is becoming increasingly attractive to employers. Not only does it save money in overhead costs, but it also provides access to a much larger pool of potential employees, giving them a greater chance to find the most suitable candidate for the job. As someone who's been working remotely for years, I can attest to the countless benefits of remote work, from cost savings to improved productivity and flexibility.

When the COVID-19 pandemic hit, remote work became more important than ever before. It enabled businesses to continue their operations while keeping their employees safe and healthy. Of course, the pandemic also highlighted some of the downsides of remote work, such as increased loneliness and social isolation. However, companies that successfully integrated remote work with their employees saw improvements in morale and job satisfaction.

For example, Dave (not his real name), an employee at one of the companies where I worked as a fractional executive, was able to navigate the challenging times of the pandemic thanks to the company's remote work policies. That was, in fact, my main role, to enable their transition in no time. Dave was a bit lost at the beginning, used to commuting and seeing his colleagues, and not too good at self-accountability.

Because we focused on the individual as much as on the new policies and culture, not only did he have more time to spend with his family, but he was also able to work more efficiently without the distractions of the office. His company provided him with the necessary resources to make the transition to remote work as smooth as possible, which helped him maintain his productivity and well-being.

As we move forward, it's important to understand the current landscape of remote work, the challenges it presents, and the opportunities it offers. While remote work may not be ideal for everyone, it can be a game-changer for businesses and employees alike, providing the freedom and flexibility to work whenever and from wherever they want.

In this chapter, we'll dive deep into the world of remote work and explore its current state. We'll examine the current challenges it presents. We'll also explore the potential opportunities remote work offers, from reduced urban congestion to increased economic opportunities for workers in rural areas.

Remote work has the potential to impact many aspects of society, from transportation and urban planning, to the job market and company culture. In this chapter, we'll examine how remote work can lead to a reduction in carbon emissions and traffic congestion by reducing the need for daily commuting. We'll also explore the economic benefits that remote work can offer, such as providing jobs and opportunities to people who might not have access to them otherwise.

But we can't ignore the challenges that come with remote work, such as maintaining communication and collaboration, ensuring data security, and addressing the potential for social isolation. These challenges require careful consideration and planning by employers, employees, and policymakers.

Throughout this chapter, we'll discuss the role that each of these groups plays in ensuring the success of remote work.

We'll explore how employers can create a remote work culture that fosters collaboration and creativity, how employees can maintain their well-being and productivity while working remotely, and how policymakers can create supportive policies and infrastructure to ensure remote work is accessible to all. With the right approach, remote work can become a sustainable and beneficial model for the future of work.

❖❖ · ·◆· · ❖❖

The concept of remote work has been around for decades, but it has gained widespread acceptance and adoption only in recent years. The COVID-19 pandemic further accelerated the shift toward remote work, as companies had to quickly adapt their operations to a remote workforce.

Tracing the evolution of virtual work, the early days of the internet saw the development of online communication tools such as email and instant messaging, allowing remote teams to communicate and collaborate more effectively. With the advancement of technology, virtual work has become even more accessible with the use of video conferencing, cloud computing, and collaboration tools. An attractive benefit for companies is that now they can tap into a wider pool of talent.

Today, remote work stands as a viable long-term option for businesses and employees. However, remote work is not without its challenges. Maintaining communication and collaboration can be difficult, and it can be challenging to maintain a company culture when everyone is working remotely.

A Current Limitation That Affects Remote Workers

The lack of proper systems for virtual work is a challenge that many remote workers, including myself, have experienced for years. LinkedIn, for example, stresses the importance of listing a physical location for a good profile. This limitation results in missed opportunities, lower-paying jobs, and poor search appearances for workers in the regions they wish to work. Additionally, workers are unable to list multiple locations or indicate they work remotely, except within the work section.

The same goes for one of the biggest freelancing job websites, Upwork. Workers are still forced to show their physical location, and you have no way to know if those workers have some or all of their clients in a different location. This raises a very interesting question: location or experience?

Navigating the Challenges of Remote Work

Remote work comes with a unique set of challenges and obstacles that need to be addressed to ensure its success. Employees and employers alike need to have the right tools and resources at their disposal. It's essential that employers establish protocols to protect data security and privacy while ensuring that employees have the technology and equipment necessary to work productively and effectively.

Maintaining employee engagement and tracking productivity and performance can be challenging in a virtual setting, but employers can take steps to address these issues. They should ensure their communication systems are reliable and up to date and that employees have access to the resources and tools they need to be productive when working from home.

Providing support and guidance to employees is also key to making remote work successful. Employers should create clear policies and procedures for dealing with any issues that may arise, and they should give employees the tools and resources they need to track their performance and measure their productivity. By doing so, employers can help their remote workers thrive and feel supported in their work.

I understand the points raised by Jason Calacanis and Brad Gerstner (2023) regarding the importance of having offices where people can be in the same room. On the other hand, there is a unique advantage that can be leveraged by native remote companies, which can organize annual gatherings and other events to bring teams together more frequently. It's also a matter of typology, as different options work for different individuals. For instance, I have been working remotely for over ten years, and during this time I have gained firsthand experience of the high level of dedication and productivity I bring to my clients. While I acknowledge that there are certain advantages to in-person interactions, the freedom that remote work affords me brings about increased happiness, sharpness, and creativity. I must remain constantly aware of everything happening in my surroundings, and if I were to have everyone situated in the same office, I fear that I might lose some of that competitive edge. On the other hand, I'm very independent and autonomous, and someone who doesn't need micromanagement. That's not the case for all workers.

Furthermore, it is vital to stress the significance of selecting individuals who are a good fit for remote work. This aspect holds great importance. Similarly, I advise founders to hire individuals who already possess the desired personality, character, and attitude, rather than attempting to train these qualities. While skills can be taught, and various aspects can be improved, it is more challenging to change one's character. If you come across someone who constantly requires micromanagement or lacks reliability when working independently, it would be best not to hire them for remote positions. Therefore, specific traits are particularly well-suited for a remote setting, in addition to the essential hard skills.

Communication and Collaboration

Due to the lack of face-to-face interaction, communication and collaboration are difficult missions to address when working remotely, but are essential for successful remote work. To ascertain that communication is effective and efficient, employers should ensure their communication systems are up to date and reliable. Additionally, they should use a variety of communication methods, such as video conferencing, instant messaging, and email, to ensure employees are able to communicate and collaborate effectively.

Effective communication is crucial for remote teams to work together seamlessly. In fact, it can make or break a company's success.

Video conferencing not only enables face-to-face conversations, but also fosters a sense of community among remote workers. Instant messaging is great for quickly reaching out to team members for a decision or quick clarification, while email is ideal for keeping a record of important conversations and tasks.

To ensure that everyone is on the same page, employers should encourage the use of collaboration tools such as Trello. These tools enable tracking of tasks and discussions, ensuring that everyone is fully informed of their responsibilities. It's also crucial for employers to provide access to reliable video conferencing software and provide guidelines on how to use it effectively (Trello, 2023).

In addition, scheduling regular check-ins and team meetings can go a long way in keeping remote workers feeling connected and engaged. When employees feel connected and supported, they are more likely to stay motivated and work collaboratively toward a shared goal.

Employee Engagement

In a remote setting, keeping employees engaged and motivated can be a challenge, but it's absolutely crucial for a successful remote work environment. Employers need to make sure their employees feel supported and valued and have the tools and resources to stay connected and engaged.

Two companies that excel in this area are Zoom and Microsoft. Zoom employees are regularly asked for feedback and suggestions, and they're provided with virtual team-building activities to help them stay connected and engaged. Zoom also offers a variety of collaboration tools to help employees stay connected and productive. At Microsoft, employees are encouraged to participate in weekly virtual meetings where they can share ideas and collaborate with each other.

Creating opportunities for employees to connect and collaborate is essential. This can be achieved through regular check-ins, team-building activities, online video conferencing, shared project management platforms, and other forms of social interaction. With a positive and engaging work environment, employees will feel more connected to their work and the team, which leads to increased productivity and job satisfaction.

Productivity and Performance

Tracking productivity and performance can be difficult when working remotely, but it is essential for ensuring the success of remote work. Employers should provide employees with the tools and resources they need to track their performance and measure their productivity and should create clear policies and procedures for dealing with any performance-related issues that may arise.

For example, at Apple, employees are provided with performance-tracking tools, such as weekly performance reviews and monthly goal-setting sessions. They are given real-time feedback and recognition, as well as access to online resources to help them be successful. Additionally, managers are encouraged to use video conferencing and virtual communication tools to stay connected with their team.

At Facebook, employees are provided with access to online courses and mentors who can provide guidance and support. The company also provides collaboration tools, such as task management and project management software, to help employees stay productive and connected. They also have a system in place to recognize and reward exemplary performance.

Overall, tracking employee performance and productivity is essential for a successful remote work environment, and employers should make sure their employees have the tools and resources they need to succeed.

Data Security and Privacy

Data security and privacy are of the utmost importance when working remotely, and employers must ensure that the necessary protocols and procedures are in place to keep employee data safe and secure.

For example, at Automattic (2020), the company behind WordPress, all data is encrypted, and advanced security measures are in place to protect employee information. This includes the use of two-factor authentication for all sensitive data, regular security system updates, and training for employees on proper security protocols. Additionally, the company also offers advanced encryption technology, such as Transport Layer Security (TLS), to further protect its data. These measures help to ensure that employee data is kept safe and secure.

Employee Support

Employee support is essential for the success of remote work, and employers should ensure their employees have access to the resources and support they need to be successful. For example, at Buffer, employees are provided with access to mental health resources, along with generous vacation policies and sabbaticals for mental and physical health (Buffer, 2022).

Additionally, employers should provide employees with access to career development resources, such as online courses and mentorships, and should create policies that allow flexibility, understanding, and support in their roles. This can include everything from flexible work hours and remote work allowances to job sharing and the ability to work from multiple locations.

At Basecamp, employees are given the flexibility to work when and where they want and are provided with access to online courses and mentorships, as well as personal time and vacation days to take care of their mental and physical health (Basecamp, 2020).

Technology and Tools

Technology is essential for remote work to be successful, and employers must ensure their employees have access to the appropriate tools and resources they need to do their job.

At Zapier, employees are provided with access to the latest technological tools, such as cloud storage and collaboration software, to help ensure that they can work effectively and efficiently (Zapier, 2020b). Additionally, employers should make sure that their employees have the necessary resources and support to use the technology and tools, including training and tutorials.

Trello, as another example, provides employees with tutorials and training materials, as well as access to technical support, to help ensure that they can make the most of the technology and tools available to them (Trello, 2020).

Finally, employers should create policies that provide employees with flexibility and support in their roles, such as job sharing and the ability to work from multiple locations.

To ensure the success of remote work, it is essential that employers and employees are aware of these challenges and take steps to address them. As the adage goes, "If you don't prepare for the storm, you can't enjoy the rainbow." With the right preparation, remote work can be a successful and enjoyable experience for both employers and employees.

⟨⟩ · · ◆ · · ⟨⟩

Remote work can be a successful model, but it requires careful planning and implementation. Companies that want to implement remote work should involve all stakeholders, provide employees with the necessary resources and support, and clearly communicate the reasons for the change.

The shift to remote work has the potential to revolutionize the way we work in a variety of ways. Not only can it make it easier for employers to fill positions and access talent from around the world, but it can also have a positive impact on urban planning and transportation, the global economy and job market, company culture and employee well-being, and society. Each will be discussed below.

The Impact of Remote Work on Urban Planning and Transportation

By reducing the need for physical office space, remote work can decrease the demand for new buildings and infrastructure. This can lead to a reduction in traffic congestion and pollution, as well as an increase in green spaces. Additionally, it can lead to decongestion in public transportation, making it easier and more convenient for people to get around.

For example, Buffer, an all-remote company, has been able to save money and resources that can be used for other purposes, like generously compensating employees. Imagine cities with pleasant transportation routes, less pollution and noise, and more room for parks and green areas.

The Impact of Remote Work on the Global Economy and Job Market

As the era of remote work emerges, an awe-inspiring transformation unfolds, revealing a world of boundless opportunities for those residing in isolated or rural areas. These individuals, often devoid of the same employment advantages enjoyed by their urban counterparts, now have a chance to find themselves on equal footing. The newfound ability to work from any corner of the globe sets the stage for an inspiring shift.

Wage disparities between regions, and unequal treatment, can be significantly reduced and talents recognized. By tapping into an expansive and diverse talent pool, organizations can unlock the full potential of a global workforce, transcending geographical boundaries and paving the way for a more equitable future. I must say, this is very inspiring and aspirational for anyone who wants to contribute to a collective better future.

For example, Basecamp, an all-remote company, was able to access a larger and more diverse pool of talent from around the world. This allowed them to fill positions quickly and easily, and to create a team of highly skilled and motivated individuals. Basecamp was among the first ones to benefit from the fruits of a remote setting. Basecamp founders Jason Fried and David Heinemeier Hansson described in depth the advantages of remote working in their book *Remote: Office Not Required*. The book details and outlines the strategies used by the founders to develop a successful remote working culture (Basecamp, 2020).

The Impact of Remote Work on Company Culture and Employee Well-being

Remote work can also have a positive impact on company culture. By breaking down traditional hierarchies and enabling employees to work more collaboratively, it can lead to increased creativity and innovation. It can also help to create a more inclusive culture, as there is less emphasis on physical presence and more focus on the quality of work being produced. This view comes from Buffer (2019), in an article discussing the benefits of remote work and how it can impact company culture, productivity, and more.

Zapier (2020a), another all-remote company, managed to create a culture of collaboration and openness, enabling employees to work together more effectively. This has resulted in an increase in creativity and innovation.

Given the demands of modern life, it's no surprise that commuting can be a significant source of stress for many of us. Therefore, the shift to remote work can also have a positive impact on employee well-being. Remote work offers an attractive solution by eliminating the daily commute and giving employees the freedom to work from anywhere they choose. This newfound flexibility not only saves precious time and cuts costs but also holds the potential to alleviate stress. Scientific research has shown that reduced commuting and increased autonomy correlate with lower levels of cortisol, the stress hormone. In short, it's one of those seemingly small yet profoundly impactful advantages that can significantly enhance our overall well-being and quality of life (Chida & Steptoe, 2008; Etzion et al., 1998).

Automattic has enabled employees to work from anywhere (Berkun, 2013), giving them the freedom to move around and experience new places (Automattic, 2019). This has had a positive impact on employee morale and well-being and has enabled the company to attract and retain top talent.

The Impact of Remote Work on Society

Ultimately, the transformative influence of remote work extends far beyond individual experiences, holding the potential to shape society at its core. It breathes life into a new era where possibilities abound, nurturing a diverse and inclusive workforce that breaks down barriers of inequality. Embracing this paradigm shift can ignite a cascade of positive outcomes that resonate deeply within our collective existence.

A dynamic solution emerges where technology and human potential together paint a vivid portrait of a society where equal opportunities flourish. This vision propels us toward a future where shared prosperity is not just a dream but a thrilling reality we can all embrace, and shared prosperity becomes a living, breathing reality. I would say that this is something to aspire to.

As we move forward into the future, it is essential that we recognize the potential of remote work and the numerous opportunities it presents. If we are able to embrace the challenges and opportunities, we can create a world in which people are free to work from anywhere, accessing a wider pool of talent and reducing inequality, unemployment, and pollution.

We can create a world in which people can access the same employment opportunities, no matter where they live, and in which companies are able to access a more diverse and inclusive workforce. With the right tools, support, and policies in place, we can make this imaginary world a reality.

<hr />

Understanding the Benefits of Being a Remote Company

Let's consider the benefits we can all enjoy from remote work:

    1. **Increased productivity.** Remote work allows em-

ployees to create their own schedule and work environment, which can lead to increased focus and productivity.

2. **Cost savings.** Remote work eliminates the need for a physical office space, which can lead to significant cost savings for a company.

3. **Access to a global talent pool.** By allowing employees to work remotely, a company can attract top talent from around the world, regardless of their location.

4. **Increased job satisfaction.** Remote work allows employees to have a better work-life balance, which can lead to increased job satisfaction.

5. **Flexibility.** Remote work offers flexibility for employees, allowing them to take care of personal responsibilities while still being able to work.

6. **Employee retention.** Remote work can help retain employees who may otherwise have to relocate or quit due to personal or family circumstances.

7. **Increased collaboration and communication.** With the use of virtual communication and collaboration tools, remote teams can still stay connected

and engaged, fostering a sense of community.

8. **Environmental benefits.** Remote work also has environmental benefits, as it reduces the need for employees to commute, which can lead to reduced carbon emissions.

9. **Diversified workforce.** Remote work allows companies to have a more diversified workforce by not limiting themselves to a specific location. This can lead to a more inclusive and varied perspective in the company.

❖❖ · ·◆· · ❖❖

The Success of Remote Work

To ensure the success of remote work, employers must provide employees with the resources, tools, and infrastructure to do their job from home. Yet, many new arrivals in the remote space forget the basic needs of their employees.

Imagine this: a remote worker on the other side of the world, equipped with an old, crash-prone laptop. Sadly, some remote workers endure such inconveniences, unwilling to jeopardize their employment. However, unknown to many, this silent struggle steals precious time and fosters a mounting sense of stress.

I would argue that during the first steps with an employee during onboarding, you should check Maslow's pyramid and see whether your employee has the necessary elements to be successful, including a proper space, appropriate lighting, a good diet, plants, and some level of fitness. All are attributes that need addressing if you want a productive, healthy, happy, and loyal employee.

In some countries, this information may be protected; the underlying message here is to foster a comprehensive understanding of your employees, considering their unique needs and circumstances. There is no one-size-fits-all solution, but embracing a personalized approach and demonstrating empathy will always yield remarkable results. By maintaining our humanity and extending a caring touch, we can forge meaningful connections and create an environment where everyone can thrive.

Policies and procedures should be in place to handle any issues that may arise, and employers must be willing to commit to the success of remote work to make it a reality. Employees must also be willing to adapt to the new environment, embracing the opportunities and challenges of working remotely. An initial open, transparent discussion about all aspects and commitments is invaluable. Keep in mind that in a remote setting, overcommunication is the norm and is advised to avoid errors and misunderstandings.

Finally, policymakers must create laws and regulations that support the growth and sustainability of remote work, enabling employers and employees to reap its benefits. One example of this has been seen in the United States, with the introduction of the Telework Enhancement Act (2010), allowing government employees to work from home.

Current and Future Technologies and Tools for Remote Work

It's difficult to predict exactly what new technologies will emerge in the future, but several areas of innovation have the potential to revolutionize the way we work remotely. Here are some technologies that are currently transforming remote work and have the potential to revolutionize it further, including their risks:

1. **Video conferencing.** Video conferencing technology has become an essential tool for remote workers to communicate and collaborate with their colleagues and clients. However, excessive reliance on video conferencing can lead to feelings of fatigue and

burnout due to constant screen time and limited face-to-face interactions.

2. **Artificial intelligence (AI).** AI-powered tools, such as virtual assistants and chatbots, can help remote workers improve communication and collaboration while also enhancing productivity. Yet, there is a concern that excessive reliance on AI may reduce human interaction and creativity, potentially leading to a lack of personal touch and innovation in remote work environments.

3. **Location-tracking technology.** Location-tracking technology can help managers monitor the whereabouts of remote workers, but it may also lead to increased pressure on workers to be available at all times and make it challenging to maintain a healthy work/life balance.

4. **Wearable technology.** Wearable technology, such as fitness trackers and smartwatches, can monitor the productivity, sleep patterns, and overall well-being of remote workers. However, it may also increase pressure on workers to prioritize work over personal well-being.

5. **Behavioral analytics.** Behavioral analytics technol-

ogy can monitor and analyze the behavior of remote workers, but it may also increase pressure on workers to conform to certain expectations and make it difficult for them to be themselves.

6. **Blockchain technology.** Blockchain technology can create tamper-proof records of work done and payments made, which can increase trust and accountability in remote work arrangements. There are some concerns about data privacy and security breaches within the blockchain network that are under a constant debate between the blockchain supporters and the skeptics.

7. **5G networks.** 5G networks provide faster internet speeds and lower latency, allowing for more seamless communication and collaboration among remote workers, but the implementation of 5G networks may raise concerns regarding potential health effects and increased vulnerability to cyberattacks.

8. **Automation.** Automation tools can increase efficiency and productivity, and reduce human error in remote work. However, there is a risk of job displacement and the need for upskilling or reskilling to adapt to the changing work landscape.

9. **Biometric authentication.** Biometric authentication can provide a higher level of security for remote access. The concerns are about privacy, and the misuse of biometric data may arise, necessitating strict safeguards and regulations.

10. **Quantum Computing.** Quantum computing can revolutionize remote work by providing new ways to process and store data, allowing for real-time analysis of large sets of data, and performing complex simulations. The complexity and limited availability of quantum computing technology may raise challenges in its widespread adoption and compatibility.

11. **Neuromorphic computing.** Neuromorphic computing mimics the way the human brain works and can enable computers to process information in a more human-like way. Ethical considerations and potential biases in decision-making algorithms need to be addressed.

12. **Robotics.** Robotics can automate repetitive tasks and provide remote assistance to workers, allowing them to focus on more complex tasks, but job displacement for certain roles and the need for workforce adjustments and retraining are a potential risk that need to be mitigated.

13. **Internet of Things (IoT).** IoT can collect and share data from interconnected devices, leading to new ways to optimize the environment and improve the well-being and productivity of remote workers. However, concerns about data security, privacy breaches, and the potential for unauthorized access to IoT devices must be addressed.

14. **Edge computing.** Edge computing can help reduce latency, improve security, and enable real-time applications for remote workers who need to access and process large sets of data, but network stability and compatibility across different devices and platforms need to be tackled.

15. **Ambient computing.** Ambient computing can allow remote workers to access information and perform tasks through natural interactions with their environment. The constant monitoring of personal spaces and potential data misuse need to be addressed.

16. **Smart workspaces.** Smart workspaces are equipped with sensors, cameras, and other technologies that can monitor and optimize the environment, improving the well-being and productivity of remote workers. Monitoring and data collection within

smart workspaces need to be carefully managed.

17. **Biotechnology.** Biotechnology can allow remote workers to control devices and computers with their brain waves, benefiting those with mobility issues. Ethical considerations and potential misuse of neurodata need to be addressed to ensure privacy and consent.

Companies and individuals need to keep an eye on these developments and think about how they can be leveraged to enhance the remote work experience.

The Future of Remote Work

The future of remote work is uncertain, and employers, employees, and policymakers must work together to ensure its success. By providing employees with the tools and resources they need to work effectively from home, and by creating policies and regulations that support the growth of remote work, employers, employees, and policymakers can ensure the success of remote work in the future.

Technologies like AI, IoT, and virtual reality can be used to create immersive virtual work environments, while the development of new technologies can enable remote workers to collaborate from anywhere in the world, accessing a wider pool of talent and creating a more diverse and inclusive workforce.

By embracing the challenges and opportunities associated with remote work, we can create a future in which people are free to work from anywhere, revolutionizing urban planning and transportation, the global economy and job market, company culture, employee well-being, and society.

References

Automattic. (2020). Security at Automattic. https://automattic.com/security/

Automattic. (2019). How we work. https://automattic.com/how-we-work/

Basecamp. (2020). Working remotely at Basecamp. https://basecamp.com/remote-resources

Berkun, S. (2013). How WordPress thrives with a 100% remote workforce. https://hbr.org/2013/03/how-wordpress-thrives-with-a-1

Buffer. (2022). Mental health resources. https://buffer.com/resources/mental-health/

Buffer. (2022). State of remote work. https://buffer.com/st
ate-of-remote-work/2022

Buffer. (2019). The state of remote work: Key trends for
2019. https://buffer.com/state-of-remote-work/2019

Calacanis J., & Gerstner B. (2023, May 20). Fireside
chat with Jason Calacanis & Brad Gerstner hosted by
Mubadala's Ibrahim Ajami | E1746. This week in star-
tups. https://www.youtube.com/watch?v=oc5tHbEK0IQ

Chida, Y., & Steptoe, A. (2008). Cortisol awak-
ening response and psychosocial factors: A systematic review and meta-analysis. *Biological Psychology, 80*(3), 265-278. doi: 10.1016/j.biopsycho.2008.03.00
6 https://www.sciencedirect.com/science/article/abs/pii/S
0301051108002202?via%3Dihub

Etzion, D., Eden, D., & Lapidot, Y. (1998). Relief from job
stressors and burnout: Reserve service as a respite. *Journal of
Applied Psychology, 83*(4), 577–585. https://doi.org/10.103
7/0021-9010.83.4.577

Fried, J., Heinemeier, H.D. (2013). *Remote: Office not required*. Vermill.

Imre, C. (2018, March 14). Remote work is
here to stay. How to find the best companies.

LinkedIn https://www.linkedin.com/pulse/remote-work-here-stay-how-find-best-companies-dr-cristina-imre/

NBER. (April, 2021). Why working from home will stick. https://www.nber.org/system/files/working_papers/w28731/w28731.pdf

Telework Enhancement Act. (2010). H.R. 1722, public law 111–292 https://www.congress.gov/111/plaws/publ292/PLAW-111publ292.pdf

Trello. (2020). *Onboarding with Trello*. https://trello.com/onboarding

Trello. (2023). *Remote teams*. https://trello.com/en/teams/remote-team-management

Zapier. (2020a). *Why Zapier has always been 100% remote*. https://zapier.com/blog/why-work-remotely/

Zapier. (2020b). *Zapier and remote work*. https://zapier.com/remote-work

Zapier Team and Foster, W. (2019). The ultimate guide to remote work. https://cdn.zapier.com/storage/learn_ebooks/b8a9bc98ff52fda88db96f92225c126c.pdf

Praise for Winning in the Virtual Workplace

"Winning in the Virtual Workplace is a winner—a treasure trove of practical wisdom on timely and significant issues! In the book, experts in the virtual workplace offer fresh insights, practical advice, and illustrative examples on topics ranging from emotional intelligence, engagement, and accountability, to communication, human capital, and continuous improvement. *Winning in the Virtual Workplace* is a collection you'll want to consult as you tackle the challenges of the new world of work. Keep it within arm's reach in your virtual workplace."

—Jim Kouzes, coauthor of the bestselling book, *The Leadership Challenge*, and a Fellow at the Doerr Institute for New Leaders, Rice University.

"*Winning in the Virtual Workplace*, curated by the Center for the Advancement of Virtual Organizations, brilliantly deciphers the complex landscape of leading in a virtual setting. With Emotional Intelligence at its core, this book provides a strategic blueprint, featuring critical components such as Communication, Engagement, and Accountability. The multi-disciplinary perspectives offered by the authors make this book an invaluable resource for leaders aiming for excellence in virtual environments. From practical tips on fostering psychological safety to strategies for mitigating proximity bias, this book offers a comprehensive and nuanced understanding of virtual leadership. It not only addresses current challenges but also lays the groundwork for ongoing innovation and continuous improvement. A must-read for anyone invested in mastering the art of virtual leadership."

—Dr. Gleb Tsipursky, CEO of Disaster Avoidance Experts and Author of *Returning to the Office and Leading Hybrid and Remote Teams*

"Leading (and working in) a virtual environment is certainly a challenge. This new book uses a form of "crowdsourcing" from renowned experts to provide strategies for leading a remote workforce. This is a must-have guide for leaders and employees who work remotely."

—Ronald E. Riggio, Ph.D., Henry R. Kravis Professor of Leadership, Claremont McKenna College

"The ten leaders featured in this book share proven techniques and strategies to assist organizational leaders in establishing successful virtual work environments. *Winning in the Virtual Workplace* serves as a guidebook, offering valuable insights for leaders seeking to create thriving virtual workplaces. From harnessing the power of virtual tools to fostering a culture of connectedness, this book is a valuable resource for those seeking to create successful teams."

—Dr. Tiffany A. Pringle, Ed.D., President of Inspire Consulting & Management Group

A Note to the Reader

A quick favor...

We hope you enjoyed this book. Ratings and reviews are important to help get the word out about books. They not only help future readers, they help out authors and publishers, too.

Could you take 1-3 minutes to leave an honest review (or simply rate the book)? A review can be as short as you like. By doing so, you would help others know the value of this book.

You can do this by returning to the website where you got the book. You can just share in a few words or sentences your thoughts about the book so others can know if it's for them, too.

Thank you!

Authors and Editors

Dr. Brian M. Allen

Brian M. Allen has more than 30 years of leadership experience in international project and operations management. His expertise includes leadership and sales experience in information technology, ecommerce, telecommunications, international sales and operations management, and international project management. His broad experience includes leading organizations and managing projects in 38 countries throughout North America, Central America, South America, Western Europe, Asia, Africa, and Australia. Dr. Allen holds a Doctor of Business Administration in Technology Entrepreneurship, an MBA, and a Master's in Project Management.

Sylvia Baffour

Sylvia Baffour is an Emotional Intelligence coach, profession-al speaker and trainer, recently ranked by HubSpot among the Top 15 female motivational speakers, alongside the likes of Oprah Winfrey and Mel Robbins. She is the author of *I Dare You to Care*. For over 18 years, she has leveraged tools and strategies from her Dare to Care™ EI Framework to help organizations build healthy work cultures with emo-tional intelligence. Clients who have benefitted from Sylvia's expertise include Whirlpool Inc., Lockheed Martin, Capital One, Doctors Without Borders, The World Bank, and the Department of Defense, to name a few. Her website is: http s://sylviaspeaks.com.

Dr. Marie Bakari

Marie Bakari has held numerous positions in higher educa-tion serving as faculty, subject matter expert, program lead, and Associate Director of Faculty Support and Development. She holds master's degrees in Business Administration and Accounting, a DBA in Multicultural Entrepreneurship, and an EdD in Education Leadership. Her research interests in-clude studies in business and cultural competence. Diversity, equity, inclusion, belonging, and social justice guide her day-to-day work with faculty and students. Dr. Bakari follows the philosophy that to teach effectively, one must continue to learn.

Elizabeth Kemp Caulder

For more than a quarter century, Elizabeth Kemp Caulder has served in leadership at agencies, leading brand strategy for the world's most recognizable brands, and building some of the industry's most effective teams. She founded THE PHOENIX Lifestyle Marketing Group on the promise and premise of remote work to support recruitment and retention of the highest caliber talent able to work from the location that makes them their happiest, most productive selves. Elizabeth is also dedicated to having her agency support brands that are resolute about creating a legacy of positive impact, allowing her team to support meaningful work that improves our world. These include partnerships with organizations like Ahold Delhaize-USA, Deloitte, EdChoice, March of Dimes, The National Football League, Peapod Digital Labs, UNIFI (The Makers of Repreve), USAA, and WM (formerly Waste Management). Despite a demanding career, Elizabeth serves her community, volunteering her time and expertise through various mentorship programs and non-profit boards. She has been honored as an Enterprising Woman of the Year, listed as one of *Inc. Magazine's* 250 Female Founders, named one of TDR's Most Admired CEOs, listed among the Top 100 Leading Women in Maryland, named one of Women We Admire's 50 Women Leaders of DC, and was a finalist in *Cosmopolitan Magazine's* The New C-Suite. Elizabeth's unique leadership has also been featured in *Inc.*, *IE*, and *CanvasRebel* magazines. Learn more at www.PhoenixLMG.com, or on social media @PhoenixLMG.

Dr. John Frame

John Frame has a DPhil from the University of Oxford and coaches part-time faculty in a fully remote environment in the School of Business and Economics at National University. His books and audiobooks are: *Homeless at Harvard; 7 Attitudes of the Helping Heart*; and a short read, *Increase Your Leadership Impact: 6 Simple Strategies to Connect with God's Wisdom, Make Tough Decisions, and Inspire Those Around You*.

Molly Gutterud

Molly Gutterud is an accomplished professional in marketing and communications, specializing in digital strategy and brand development. With 15+ years of experience, Molly consistently drives brand awareness and customer engagement. She excels in leading successful marketing campaigns, leveraging her expertise in content marketing. Her data-driven approach and analytics skills yield actionable insights for optimizing marketing efforts and maximizing ROI. Molly is recognized for building strong client relationships and fostering long-term partnerships based on trust and success. Her exceptional leadership inspires cross-functional teams to deliver outstanding results. Molly is a sought-after speaker and industry contributor, sharing expertise on the evolving marketing and communications landscape.

Nadia Harris

Nadia Harris, LLM, MBA is founder of remoteworkadvocate.com, and an international remote and hybrid work expert, keynote speaker, university lecturer, and author of numerous flexible working publications, including her book, *How to Tackle Hybrid Working*. She's a leader in remote and hybrid work, and has been acknowledged in the TOP 15 Remote Work Advocates and Who's Who in Remote Working. During her professional career, she has worked with numerous international companies – both start-ups and structured corporations, where she has successfully implemented frameworks to ensure the scalability of flexible working models. She's fluent in English, German, Polish, and French. Nadia holds a legal degree, specializing in remote work law, and an MBA in Intercultural Managerial Communication.

Dr. Cristina Imre

Cristina Imre is a pioneering figure in transformative leadership and remote work. As the founder of Tech Leadership Lab, she combines her expertise as an entrepreneur, executive coach, fractional executive, and author to foster technological innovation and global change. She is now on an audacious mission to accelerate the resolution of the 17 SDGs. With nearly two decades of experience, she guides leaders in creating effective virtual workplaces and advocates for equitable remote work. Cristina offers a unique perspective on creating successful virtual workplaces around the globe. Beyond her professional realm, Cristina's influence extends to advocating for non-biased remote work, empowering individuals globally, regardless of their location, age, gender, or sexual orientation. Her website is https://cristinaimre.com.

Linda Larsen

Linda Larsen is an experienced project manager with nearly two decades of service in program and project management for nonprofit, higher education, and international organizations. Her expertise includes leading end-to-end program delivery, strategic planning, process improvement, workflow optimization, operations management, marketing strategies and bridging intercultural relationships. An avid supporter of virtual work and a lifelong learner, she is fluent in Mandarin Chinese and holds a master's degree from George Washington University, as well as a bachelor's degree from University of California, Los Angeles.

Anand Madhavan

Anand Madhavan grew up in Lincoln, NE and earned his undergraduate degree at the University of Nebraska-Lincoln, in Marketing. After moving to Omaha, NE and working full-time, he completed an MBA at the University of Nebraska-Omaha with an emphasis in International Business. He's worked in the field of digital marketing for the last 18 years and is now the Director of Digital Strategy for Gallup. He leads a group of analysts and subject matter experts that are responsible for reviewing analytics and digital strategy that has led to meeting important goals of the organization. He is blessed with two beautiful daughters – Alliyah, age 10, and Avani, age 8. They have made Omaha their home.

Catherine Mattiske

Catherine Mattiske is best known for inventing ID9 Intelligent Design, as well as the Genius Quotient (GQ). She's a leading light in the corporate learning and team building industries. Catherine regularly works with large and small organizations to help team members better understand one another, while effectively collaborating and boosting employee morale and productivity. Since having started her business, The Performance Company, she has spent nearly three decades serving clients globally in dozens of different industries. She helps them change their behavior, strengthen teams, and see promising results. If one person on this planet knows how to help people become more influential in less time, it is her! Catherine is a woman of many words, with a strong belief in the value behind unlocking our learning and communication preferences to connect better, all while becoming the most powerful version of ourselves. She uses her hands-on experience and knowledge to provide individuals with tips, tricks, and other tools based on their archetypes. She has written and published 31 books, including a 27-part short series and other top-rated reads, such as *Train for Results*; *Training Activities That Work*; *Leading Virtual Teams,* and her latest, *Unlock Inner Genius*. Learn more about Catherine's services and resources, by visiting her website at: https://thegeni usquotient.com. You can connect with Catherine through LinkedIn.

Dr. Stephanie Menefee

Stephanie Menefee is Founder and Owner of Floreo Collective, LLC, a consulting firm specializing in leadership development, assessing organizational environments, developing data-driven initiatives with measurable goals, providing alternative dispute resolution services, and facilitating interactive leadership and team building workshops. Dr. Menefee is also an experienced higher education administrator, professor, and conference speaker. A certified conflict resolution practitioner with backgrounds in administration and psychology,

Dr. Menefee's current research centers on dispute resolution, collaboration, and creativity in on-ground, remote, and hybrid public sector teams.

Dr. William J. Quinn, III

William Quinn is an operations and project management professional with over 25 years of experience in the field of manufacturing. Throughout his career, Dr. Quinn has focused on the principles of good leadership. As a result, he has mentored several current and future leaders in a variety of industries. He holds a BS in Chemical Engineering from the New Jersey Institute of Technology, a Doctor of Business Administration from Northcentral University, and has recently completed a Technical Project Management Program at the Massachusetts Institute of Technology. You can reach William through LinkedIn.

Dr. Melody Rawlings

Melody Rawlings is the Director of the Center for the Advancement of Virtual Organizations at National University, and a doctoral chair in the School of Business and Economics.

She has over 10 years of remote and hybrid team experience and has authored peer-reviewed publications on topics such as leadership development, remote teamwork, emotional intelligence, eService learning, imposter phenomenon, and student philanthropy. Along with Dr. Kimberly Janson, she co-authored *Determining Leadership Potential: Powerful Insights to Winning at the Talent Game*.

Dr. Kathy Richie

Kathy Richie is an Associate Professor at National University. She primarily teaches leadership, management strategy, and change management online courses at the master's and doctoral level, in addition to actively serving on student dissertation committees. Her background blends academic practice with business acumen to represent real-world views. She has many years of hands-on remote work experience managing teams across the U.S. as a corporate account negotiator for a large multinational high-tech corporation. Dr. Richie continued the virtual experience by completing her doctorate degree online. Her dissertation research focused on how organizational culture is affected when teams work remotely alongside on-site employees.

Dr. Randee L. Sanders

Randee L. Sanders is the Founder of RL Sanders & Associates. She is a women's career strategist, speaker, and the Associate Dean of Faculty at the School of Business and Economics at National University. She has an affinity for advancing highly ambitious professional women leaders into positions of leadership and influence. Through her Design Not Default Academy, Dr. Randee consults with women leaders to establish a strong sense of self, develop individual voice, and generate new strategies to develop their effectiveness, influence, talent, and power to lead. Dr. Randee is passionate about educating the next generation of leaders in business and higher education. She enjoys creating positive energy, passionate synergies, and transforming people's lives. She believes that the time is now to live your fabulous life!

Lauren Sergy

Lauren Sergy is a communication expert specializing in workplace interpersonal communication and public speaking skills. She has delivered keynotes and workshops across Canada, the US, the UK, and beyond, helping thousands of people become more effective leaders through skilled communication. Her clients include companies such as 3M, KPMG, Cargill, T-Mobile, and others. Lauren holds a Masters in Library and Information Studies, a Bachelor of Arts, and a Certificate in Management Development. She has taught business communication at the University of Alberta and Concordia University of Edmonton, is a regular guest lecturer at other post-secondary institutions, and has made many appearances on radio and television. Lauren has authored two books, *The Handy Communication Answer Book* (named on Library Journal's *Best Reference 2017 list)* and *UNMUTE! How to Master Virtual Meetings and Reclaim Your Sanity*. To learn more about Lauren's services and resources, visit her website at http://www.LaurenSergy.com.

Dr. Gary White

Gary White is a Professor of Business and Leadership, and Chair of doctoral dissertations at National University. He is the Academic Program Director for the Master of Science in Organizational Leadership Program. He also serves as co-chair of the National Society for Leadership Success (NSLS) honor society. He has been involved in higher education for over 30 years, teaching business, management, marketing, organizational leadership, and quantitative and

statistical analysis at several universities. He has won numerous awards and recognition for teaching excellence and is a
two-time Lindback Distinguished Teaching Award nominee.
Since 1991, he's been the owner of a small business consulting
firm. Dr. White has a B.A. in Environmental Sciences from La
Salle University, an M.S. in Organizational Dynamics from
the University of Pennsylvania, and a Ph.D. in Educational
Leadership and Systems, with a specialization in Marketing
and Higher Education, from Union Institute University.

Geraldine Woloch-Addamine

Geraldine Woloch-Addamine is the Founder & CEO at
Good4work, a Total Talent Recognition software with a mission to harness the power of Web 3 to increase Team/Em-
ployee Engagement by recognizing and rewarding talents. She
is French and lived in Paris before moving to San Francis-
co in 2014 with her family. She provides thought leadership
to inspire managers and leaders to build a high-performing
culture of trust. Geraldine draws her inspiration and expertise from her stories of navigating for 15 years the corporate
world in France and the US. She's served as a Manager, HR
Business Partner, and now as a global leader in the high-tech
sector. Her primary focus has been on building new projects,

teams, and products in Talent/Performance Management, while supporting leaders. Geraldine holds a Master in HR from Sciences Po Paris and an HR certificate from UC Berkeley Extension.

Stay in Touch

Want to continue learning about how to be a first-class leader of remote and hybrid employees? Stay in touch with the Center for the Advancement of Virtual Organizations.

National University's Center for the Advancement of Virtual Organizations (CAVO) is a hub of relevant resources providing current information and practices to support professionals and educators in various industries involved in remote work. Serving as a collaborative platform, CAVO partners with remote work experts to integrate research and practical knowledge, with the goal of disseminating the latest developments and technologies associated with remote work. For podcast episodes and other resources to help you lead a virtual organization, please visit: https://www.nu.edu/center-advancement-virtual-organizations.

www.ingramcontent.com/pod-product-compliance
Lightning Source LLC
Chambersburg PA
CBHW020149090426
42734CB00008B/753